ALL IN THE
FAMILY

THE EBB AND FLOW OF FAMILIES IN BUSINESS

Curated by Jennifer Bright, Rita Guthrie, and Robert Sayre
Photographs by Terree O'Neill Oakwood
LEHIGH VALLEY EDITION

©2024 Bright Communications LLC

Internet addresses given in this book were accurate
at the time it went to press.

Printed in the United States of America

Published in Hellertown, PA

Cover and interior design and illustrations by Christina Gaugler

Photographs on pages 15, 20, 27, 32, 39, 44, 51, 63, 68, 87, 104, 111, 116, 123, 124 by Terree O'Neill Oakwood

ISBN 978-1-958711-97-2

Library of Congress Control Number 2023924265

Bright
COMMUNICATIONS

To my family business—and to yours
—Jennifer Bright

*To my business clients and colleagues who believe
that my ideas and expertise made them better: It's the
other way around. Your energy, your knowledge, your
encouragement, and your connections shaped me.
To our contributors: By sharing your stories, you elevate
our entire community and help other entrepreneurs
envision how they too can rock the world.*
—Rita Guthrie

*To our contributors: Families are the core building blocks
for societies in all cultures and nations. Likewise, small
businesses are positioned in the economy in the same
way. While the stock market and commodity prices in
the Midwest are reported on daily, the real heartbeat of
a community can be found in the family-owned small
businesses. They provide employment for members of
their family, and they also volunteer for, donate to, and
invest in their local communities. Without them, America
would not be the same. The ones profiled here are stellar
examples of these virtues.*
—Robert Sayre

Contents

Introduction

After creating two collaborative books about local small businesses, it became clear to me that there are so many diverse, successful family businesses in our community. I wanted us to shine a light on them.

We have chosen to welcome back a few of our prior contributors to tell their story from a different angle along with their family members because there's so much more to delve into.

Most of us did not set out to change the world. Whether our business journey began on a farm or on a college campus, the common thread is that we have each learned how to grow a business while managing from the heart.

What determines our success? Perhaps a simple desire to do better than the previous generation. Most of us have explored multiple paths, looking for the golden combination of professional satisfaction while still being able to feed our families.

We cannot and do not go it alone. Innovation, relationships, and experiences impact us along the way.

In these pages, I see creativity and community, connections and courage, control and confidence. While chaos and confusion can temporarily derail our forward motion, that is often what propels us into innovation and exploration, and we rise up even stronger than before.

—Rita Guthrie

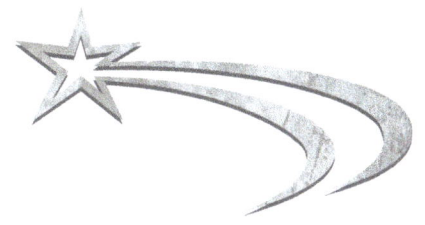

When we were brainstorming for a title and a focus for the third book in our Local Luminaries series, we came up with All in the Family. I chuckled a little and thought of Archie Bunker and his wife Edith from the TV show of the same name. Families are where are deepest connections are found. Our deepest love and hope reside here.

How important are small, family-owned business enterprises? They are at the heart of the US economy. The Small Business Association (SBA) notes, "There are more than 33 million small businesses in the United States. They employ 61.7 million Americans, totaling 46.4 percent of private sector employees. From 1995 to 2021, small businesses created 17.3 million net new jobs, accounting for 62.7 percent of the jobs created since 1995."

According to the Family Firm Institute, "Only 30 percent of family businesses survive into the second generation, 12 percent survive into the third generation, and only 3 percent operate into the fourth generation or beyond." Most of the family-owned business profiled in this book are in the process of teaching the second generation the business or hope to. While the business is often not the core of the family relationships, they do provide unique opportunities and challenges.

A business enterprise can be likened to a planet revolving around the sun. When we think of companies like Amazon, Microsoft, Apple and Walmart, we cannot forget that these were all formed by people and families—in the case of Amazon husband and wife and Walmart multi-generation.

Small, family-owned businesses are the bedrock of almost all small to mid-sized towns in the United States. The ones profiled here are no different. They represent freedom, opportunity, grit, and hard work. Their stories inspired us, and I think they will inspire you as well.

—Robert Sayre

Adam Gangewere (right) and Elizabeth Ortiz (left), with their daughters Eva, Emma, and Elyse (middle left to right), proudly serve guests from their new Emmaus location and food truck

Cactus Blue

Serving Up Creative Flavors from Puebla to Pennsylvania

One late summer day in 2004 Adam Gangewere was working as an executive chef for a food service management company in the Lehigh Valley. On his drive home that day he called his then-fiancée, Elizabeth Ortiz to say, "I think we should open our own restaurant." Elizabeth immediately hung up on him. In retrospect, that moment was the beginning of their entrepreneurial journey.

Gangewere grew up in the restaurant business. His mother owned a pizzeria during his high school and college days. After high school, Adam decided to further his education by enrolling in a culinary school based out of Pittsburgh, where he trained as a chef. He later graduated from Widener University with a bachelor's degree in Hospitality Management.

"I was completely shocked," she said. "I thought we were set—exactly where we wanted to be at that time in our lives. We both grew up in loving but humble homes. I was the first in my family to go to college, and at the time I thought we were both working in our dream jobs. I thought, *You're going to chef, and I'm going to teach. For life. That's the plan*. I like to have a plan. I was surprised that Adam wanted to rock the boat."

Elizabeth, a professor at Cedar Crest College at the time, wasn't ready for the bigger boat Adam envisioned.

When Adam called back, or when she called him—neither really remembers at this point—Elizabeth apologized and was intrigued to hear him out. He explained that although he liked the company he worked for and the people he cooked for, the meals he prepared felt prescribed: one teaspoon of this, one tablespoon of that. He felt limited. Stifled

Elizabeth knew the sobering stats that 80 percent of new restaurants fail within five years, but she took a few tentative steps toward Adam. She said, "I can tell you're excited about this, but I need to see it on paper." She had to get caught up with him in her own way.

So the couple sat down together and began planning. Serendipitously, Elizabeth was teaching a class at Cedar Crest College that required her

"Adam is six-foot-six-inches tall, and he dishes up the amount of food that he would want to eat. We don't want someone to get home and be hungry for a snack. In fact, they'll probably leave with a to-go box." —Elizabeth Ortiz

students write business plans. Right alongside her students, Elizabeth wrote her own plan for their restaurant, and as she wrote, she could see the vision coming together.

A first critical decision was what type of cuisine the restaurant would serve. Adam and Elizabeth researched and learned that the most popular types of restaurants in the Lehigh Valley at the time were Italian, Chinese, and Mexican, in that order. The Mexican restaurants at the time were either large chains or delicious mom-and-pop operations that often had limited hours, which they knew offered an opportunity. Plus, Adam had grown up working in his mom's pizzeria with a talented chef named Casimiro Linares-Sanchez, who grew up in Puebla, Mexico—the exact flavor profile Adam wanted to build his menu around. Adam invited Millo to join their operation, and when Millo accepted it validated their plan.

Next, Adam and Elizabeth began looking for their restaurant's location. "Property owners were not eager to rent to two twenty-five-year-olds, first-time restauranteurs," they remembered. Time after time, they were turned down. Finally, the owner of a space in a small shopping center just off Route 22 on Schoenersville Road took a chance on them.

Elizabeth backed Adam's optimism up with more planning and preparation. She went to the Lehigh University Small Business Development Center for their advice and expertise. (Many years later, Elizabeth has almost completed her PhD in Teaching, Learning and Technology there, too.)

Armed with confidence and a plan, they next tried to secure a loan—despite having the backing of the Small Business Development Center, no bank would offer two twenty-five-year-old first-time restauranteurs a loan. But Adam's mother, Bonnie, believed in them so much that she invested in their restaurant.

"She knew her son was onto something," Elizabeth said. (A few years later, when the couple gave Bonnie their last repayment of that loan, they all celebrated with champagne.)

Then, in October 2004, Adam and Elizabeth finally began extensive renovations of their new restaurant space.

"Elizabeth's parents, Boby and Susan, their friends, and extended family chipped in their time and gave us a hand with the renovations as we quickly approached our projected opening date," said Adam. Every night after work for three months, the group met at the restaurant to paint, tile and get the restaurant set up for the first day in business. It was a group effort and a true labor of love that would not have come to fruition without the support. .

Along the way, Adam and Casimiro started to created the restaurant's menu. Of course, it featured plenty of Puebla-inspired dishes, including chili rellenos, tamales and enchiladas. Also on the menu were popular dishes from both countries like tacos, quesadillas, and burritos.

"From the beginning, they made everything from scratch. Freshness matters and the kitchen staff worked hard to ensure that the flavors are always on point." Elizabeth related.

Excited, Adam and Elizabeth began promoting their grand opening. But first, the restaurant needed a name! Like many great brainstorming sessions, they tossed around ideas. In the car one day, they agreed that the name was to have the word "Cactus" in it. Tossing around a few words trying to make something fit they came up with the word "Blue"

Blue Cactus? That sounded good but not great. They tried other colors and eventually Adam decided to flip the two words around. How about Cactus Blue?

The beginning of December 2004 came quickly and they finally had the restaurant painted, decorated and furnished. The kitchen equipment was in place, food supplies were starting to come in and they were starting to hire staff (mainly their friends at the time). After passing all the necessary inspections, including health, fire and building the two restauranteurs were ready to host their soft opening walk through with family and friends.

Word started to spread about the new restaurant opening, media outlets like the Morning Call and Lehigh Valley Style picked up their story. The couple was set to open the door to the public for the first time two days after Christmas.

Day one, the guacamole was made, the verde sauce blended from scratch and the Mexican rice was prepped. In came the first customer, an elderly Pennsylvania Dutch woman that lived next door. "We didn't mind that she ordered a hot dog and French fries off the children's menu, we were excited to have our first customer in the books," said Adam. He continued, "We were happy to serve a few customers on day one, a few more on day two and each day after more and more guests began to dine with us. Eventually we began to serve regulars and many of them became friends."

In 2004, the restaurant opened with thirteen tables, but in 2008 they expanded into the space next door and upped their table count to twenty. Over the years, Cactus Blue has weathered many storms—financial crises, housing crashes, and a global pandemic. Each time, they drew on their strengths.

Like many restaurants during the Covid-19 pandemic, they were able to keep the lights on by offering take-out and delivery. They also innovated by creating new family meals, such as make your own fajitas and enchilada bakes. During the pandemic, customers could pull up outside the restaurant, pop open their trunks and the Cactus Blue team would contactlessly deliver the meals to their vehicles.

The most popular item on the Cactus Blue menu is their Fish Tacos. "It's good for you comfort food," Elizabeth explained—battered cod with their special baja sauce. In addition to their dine-in restaurant, Cactus Blue has a thriving take-out business, delivery, and a food truck!

"When you roll up to a location in a food truck, you are greeted by such pure joy," Elizabeth said. "The food truck community in the Lehigh Valley is incredibly tight-knit. It's not competitive. It's collaborative," continued Adam. Having the food truck has led to so many opportunities for the restaurant and they would love to add another to continue to be able to serve the increased demand.

Cactus Blue also offers catering. The most popular catering item is their fajita bar, which includes plenty of tortillas, shredded beef, shredded chicken, grilled vegetables (poblano peppers, onions, and tomatoes) and toppings such as cheese, lettuce, pico de gallo, guacaomole, and sour cream. Guests build their own fajitas, which are completely customizable to suit vegetarians, vegans, and those with even the most particular tastes.

The portions of the fajita bar fall in line with all the dishes at Cactus Blue. The family's goal is no guest leaves hungry.

"Adam is six-foot-six-inches tall, and he dishes up the amount of food that he would want to eat," Elizabeth said. "We don't want someone to get home and be hungry for a snack. In fact, they'll probably leave with a to-go box."

After eighteen years of successful business in Bethlehem on Schoenersville Road, Adam and Elizabeth decided to make a move across the Lehigh Valley, to a location closer to their home and the busy extracurricular lives of their three daughters.

The new location, at 4030 Chestnut Street in Emmaus, was designed to feel like a permanent food truck. While their full-time and part-time staff were invited to make the move with them, the smaller, more intimate space with counter service for ten tables requires fewer front-of-the-house staff, but the kitchen is busier than ever. They offer family meals, to-go, and catering for small and large, and even very large events. (Think warehouses feeding their entire staff of thousands for a holiday or company milestone.) During the warmer months they add tables outside, and they staff the food truck for nearly nine months out of the year.

"Even after the pandemic, many families seem to prefer getting their food to go and eating in the comfort of their own homes," Adam said. "Times will continue to change, and we will be sure to meet the continuing needs of those that support us and the entire team at Cactus Blue, are delighted and honored to serve them.

Secrets to Our Success

Find your niche. From the beginning, Adam and Elizabeth identified the cuisine they thought would resonate with Lehigh Valley customers. They were right, and they have stuck to that proven concept.

Role with it. Their success in working together can be attributed to their distinct but complementary roles. Adam's focus on operations ensures the restaurant runs smoothly, while Elizabeth's efforts to maintain a strong online and community presence help attract and engage customers.

Give back. Their shared commitment to local community organizations adds a meaningful and impactful dimension to their lives and business, fostering a sense of purpose and community engagement that has come back to them tenfold.

For More Information

- www.cactusblue.biz

- 610-814-3000

- info@cactusblue.biz

- 4030 Chestnut Street, Emmaus, PA 18049

- Services offered: Dine-in, takeout, catering, private parties, food truck

Savory Grille

We Treat the Lehigh Valley to Special Savory Fare

Lehigh Valley natives and high school sweethearts Dorothy and Shawn Doyle met at Salisbury High School and Lehigh County Vo-Tech.

"The other students looked up to Shawn because he already had restaurant experience, having started working at his uncle's restaurant at age twelve," Dorothy remembered. "Even back then, he had an incredible talent for cooking. He was put on this earth to be a chef."

Though Dorothy remembered one day Shawn showed her how to use the pressure cooker, burning himself in the process. "That definitely caught my attention!" she said.

After the couple graduated from high school in 1983, Shawn worked for a few years at the Spring Valley Inn with Steve Kirschner, who today owns Twisted Olive. (See page 104.) They spent five years there together.

"Back in the '80s, Shawn and Steve were both busting their butts and having a great time in the restaurant business," Dorothy said. "Shawn has always been driven and motivated. He worked hard and learned a lot, working the line and also doing inventory and ordering. But then, he pours his heart into everything he does."

During high school, Dorothy worked at the long-gone Center Valley Inn. After their high school graduation, she began working at Luther Crest retirement community. It was much smaller back then, so she had the opportunity to work in all facets of the kitchen. The baker was making $1.25 more an hour than the kitchen staff. So when she left, Dorothy moved over to her job.

"I still made $4.17 an hour, since I was young and not as experienced. That's when I realized I needed to go to college and get a degree," Dorothy remembered. "That was my motivation to go away to school." Dorothy attended the Culinary Institute of America in Hyde Park, New York, a beautiful school on the banks of the Hudson River. By the time she graduated, she didn't want to be a chef or a restaurant owner.

"So, I became both," Dorothy laughed.

At right: Shawn and Dorothy Doyle, Owners of Savory Grille

In the summer of 1986, she started working at Manor House Inn, in Center Valley, working in the "back of the house" as a sous chef. Manor House was owned by a husband-and-wife team, and Dorothy worked with the wife, who became an excellent mentor.

"She was really talented," Dorothy said. "Watching her instilled drive and motivation in me to thrive, to succeed."

While Shawn was executive chef at Brookside Country Club, they started a family. Their daughter was born in 1994, and their son arrived in 1996. That's about when Shawn started planting seeds about another joint venture—their own restaurant.

"I was hesitant because I know when you own your own business, it consumes your life," Dorothy said. "At the time, our kids were really young—one and three years old. After several discussions, Shawn finally convinced me."

In 1997, the couple sold everything they owned, including their twin home in Allentown, and plunged it all into an old bar in Seisholtzville, a little village on the outskirts of Macungie.

The team at Savory Grille prepares delicious savory dishes.

They had wisely searched for a property they could afford without an investor. The building itself was small, but it was located on three acres of land. That was appealing because Dorothy and Shawn had both grown up in Lehigh County with fresh air and places to play—and they wished the same for their children. So, the family moved into the apartment upstairs from the restaurant, where they lived for the next 11 years.

When the couple bought the restaurant in October 1997, they worked tirelessly for eight weeks to make it guest ready. The old stone hotel building needed major renovations, so family and

"As a business owner, you have to be constantly updating and improving. You can't get stagnant. Keep moving forward. Keep thinking. Keep creating."

—Dorothy Doyle

friends pitched in to help gut it, move stairwells, install a commercial kitchen, and even assemble the tables and chairs. It was literally a family affair.

Meanwhile, Dorothy was still working full-time at the Manor House Inn, where she had risen to executive chef. Shawn focused on ordering all of the equipment and setting up vendors.

"With Shawn's organization skills, it all came together well."

With the restaurant gearing up to open, the couple did a massive direct-mail campaign in December of 1997, creatively using a Christmas card theme.

"We figured people don't throw out Christmas cards unopened, so these cards would get their attention," Dorothy explained.

After countless hours of work, Savory Grille opened in December 1997. While brainstorming about what to call it, a friend suggested Savory, meaning deliciously full of flavor. Shawn added Grille.

"We served twenty-eight people that first night, and we never looked back," Dorothy said. When she sees photos from that time, she's amazed, and her heart fills with pride and joy.

Both Dorothy and Shawn had a dedicated clientele from past restaurants, and those fans willingly followed them to their new restaurant-home.

From the beginning, the restaurant knew—and remained true to—its identity: fine dining. The menu is a creative blending of Shawn and Dorothy's favorite, signature dishes. Unlike many restaurants, one thing Savory Grille doesn't have is daily specials.

"Everything we serve is special!" Dorothy explained.

Over the years, the Savory Grille menu format has remained the same. It's a one-page menu that changes all the time, featuring the freshest, highest-quality ingredients—locally sourced whenever possible. One of their most popular dishes is scallops, though Dorothy's favorite is the duck breast. And their kids' favorite is the lamb.

At Savory Grille, guests enjoy their inspired takes on French, African, Asian, Mediterranean, and Southwestern cuisines.

Their bar, especially a few of its staple drinks, is extremely popular too. The bar menu also changes with the seasons. For example, some popular drinks are mint mojitos in summer, appletinis in fall, muddled old fashioneds in winter, and fruity bellinis in spring.

Because the family lived upstairs, over the years the Doyle children often made appearances at the restaurant, having pitched in from around age eight.

"One Valentine's Day weekend, our dishwasher didn't show up for work," Dorothy said. "I went upstairs and told my kids, 'Welcome to the restaurant business.' They came down to help wash dishes."

Today, their daughter, Emily, is a local hair stylist, and their son, Liam, is a geologist in Alaska.

As the Savory Grille team looks to the future, they hope to continue to grow. In particular, they are building a new greenhouse to grow their own fresh herbs, microgreens, and vegetables.

After a usual busy, long day,

Dorothy never needs to ask Shawn

"How was your day?"

"I just worked all day with him.

I know how his day was!"

—Dorothy Doyle

"As a business owner, you have to be constantly updating and improving," Dorothy said. "You can't get stagnant. Keep moving forward. Keep thinking. Keep creating."

With that philosophy always top-of-mind, Dorothy and Shawn just celebrated Savory Grille's twenty-sixth anniversary. Here's to twenty-six more!

Secrets to Our Success

Be efficient. "We work hard to reduce waste," Dorothy said. "Shawn and I have the ability to use our products effectively and efficiently. Not wasting product makes a big difference in a business's bottom line."

Be self-sufficient. Shawn and Dorothy didn't want to partner with investors, instead maintaining all control of their business.

"Being working owners, we are involved in every aspect of our business—from inventory to ordering, yard work to paperwork," Dorothy said.

Have a clear division of labor. Working with family can be challenging. One system that works well for the Doyles is their division of labor. These days, Dorothy mainly works "front-of-the-house" in the dining room, while Shawn is "back-of-the-house" in the kitchen.

Even with that distinction, after a usual busy, long day, Dorothy never needs to ask Shawn "How was your day?"

"I just worked all day with him," she said. "I know how his day was!"

For More Information

- https://savorygrille.com

- 610-845-2010

- savorygrille@gmail.com

- 2934 Seisholtzville Road,
  Macungie, PA 18062

- Services offered: Dinner only; reservations recommended

Art and Sarah Mattes, Owner and Business Manager of AWM Carpentry

AWM Carpentry

We Create Spaces You'll Love

"Art and I met at Elizabethtown College in the cafeteria line," remembered Sarah Mattes, business manager at AWM Carpentry. "It was the late 1990s, and I was studying math, and Art majored in computer science. We became fast friends, though we didn't date until our senior year."

In 2003, the couple married and settled for a while in the Harrisburg area, where Sarah enjoyed her work as a teacher. The early 2000s were tough for computer science majors, however, and Art had a hard time finding a job in his field.

Instead, he returned to his roots. His father had worked in the construction industry, beginning in radon remediation then expanding into his own general construction business. Art Mattes had worked by his dad's side as his mentee starting at age 13.

Art found a job with an Amish builder in Lancaster County. It was hard work with long hours—and a long commute.

"He was a great employer," said Art, now owner of AWM Carpentry. "We worked 6 am to 5 pm every day, plus I had to take the Amish workers to and from work because they didn't drive. The entire crew was Amish—except for me and one other person. They could use a generator and electric tools, but they wouldn't use anything connected to the electrical grid. Their goal is self-sufficiency, so they don't want to be dependent on the grid. They don't want technology to get in the way of their life and values."

"Art really enjoyed that work," Sarah said. "But that's part of his personality. He enjoys what he's doing whether that's working or doing sports. He has that grit—like his dad."

In 2005, Art and Sarah began thinking about starting a family. That is when the idea of moving back home to the Lehigh Valley took shape.

"We wanted to raise a family near our parents," Sarah said. "Plus, the Lehigh Valley is beautiful and vibrant, with so many nooks and crannies and small towns to explore."

Art took a job with a contractor in the Lehigh Valley, installing finish carpentry for new luxury homes. This was the right move for him to integrate back into the industry, network, and hone his skills. He also met a lot of people who became contacts, and he built relationships with other contractors.

"Most of those projects were $1 million-plus," Art recalled. "The trimming is the finishing crew. We hung interior doors, fashioned base moldings, and installed finishes such as wainscoting and crown molding. It's a neat process because we get to see the blank canvas of the home come to life."

The couple welcomed their first child in 2007 and their second in 2009. While Sarah was still home on maternity leave, deciding whether or not to return to teaching, she made the difficult decision to become a stay-at-home mom. Although she loved being a teacher, she wanted to be home with their children more. Within a few short weeks of making that major life choice, Art was unexpectedly laid off.

"On paper, it didn't look like we would survive financially," Art said. But somehow they did.

That's when a dream of an idea began to form in Art and Sarah's minds: starting their own business. It was born out of necessity, but it was also something that Art had thought about for a long time.

Looking back, all that turmoil might have been a blessing in disguise. "I enjoyed teaching, but I was unsatisfied, unfulfilled," Sarah said. "I really always wanted to be a full-time mom. But Art needed to work. One of the contractors he had come to know really encouraged Art. He saw leadership and entrepreneurship potential and recommended that Art start his own business. 'I'll help keep you busy!' the contractor encouraged him."

In 2010, Art and Sarah formed Arthur W. Mattes Jr Carpentry. Not only was he getting work from that contractor, but he was also getting work from new customers he had found on his own.

Art also had the opportunity to join forces with a friend who had also been laid off from his construction job. The pair began working together, as sole proprietors supporting each other—running their businesses in parallel. That went on for years. By 2016, Art's business had grown enough to warrant hiring its first carpenter employee.

When their youngest, of now three children, started school in 2019, Sarah began learning some of the tasks and roles that she could fill. In 2020, Sarah officially joined the company, now known as AWM Carpentry, LLC. She became its business manager, doing admin work, being the first point of contact for customers, and working on marketing.

"I tried to help Art where I could. But once our daughter started school, I really began to step into this new career opportunity for myself and became more supportive of our family business."

"One of the things that sets us apart from other contractors in the Lehigh Valley is when you call, I answer," Sarah said. "Often, when you call a contractor you get voicemail because the contractor is *working* on the job site. I think that people appreciate when they call our office, they get to talk with someone right away." Sarah and Art are striving to make the customer experience with their carpentry service exceptional.

Business was zipping along at a great, steady pace for AWM Carpentry until a few short months into 2020. The pandemic. And the shutdown. Carpenters were not deemed essential, so their company was shut down at the end of March and it stayed closed through the entire month of April.

"It was very scary—we had *no* income," Art said.

But the pandemic offered a silver lining.

"It gave us the opportunity to carve out space and time to work on and

Cabinetry and millwork by AWM Carpentry

think *about* our business," Art said. "I read a lot, took courses, and even trained with online business coaches."

"That time sent us down entirely new avenues of learning," Sarah said. And the couple has enjoyed tremendous growth ever since.

In 2020, the company began focusing more on its website, Search Engine Optimization, and digital advertising. Happily, not much advertising is required, though, because their top-quality work speaks for itself. Customers eagerly recommend them to others—and hire them for repeat jobs.

One particular trend in the home-building industry greatly benefitted AWM: the penchant of builders to build the same house, or close to it, over and over and over in a development.

"People want to customize their home to suit their personality," Sarah said. "They don't want a boring, vanilla home just like their neighbor's house. For example, recently, a couple that moved into a 55-plus community filled with similar houses hired us to add a coffered ceiling, a TV surround, and decorative framing on their walls."

"Those are our favorite type of clients," Art added. "They understand the value in our work. People who are building a home get burned out working for such a long time with the builder, and they might be skeptical about paying extra costs for custom work. They often complete the build, then they feel more control over the process and budget by starting fresh with us to customize their home. Plus, we offer a higher level of craftsmanship."

Also, the type of projects AWM Carpentry specializes in add functionality to a home. "We can help families figure out how to better use their space," Sarah said. "We build permanent, beautiful storage solutions."

Shelves are a better storage option than piles, and cabinets with doors are better yet. "Customers often say, 'I want doors on this because I don't want to see what's behind them,'" Sarah said.

AWM's craftsmanship adds interest, beauty, and value to a home. "When we meet with clients, we give them wisdom and options," Sarah said. "We offer a lot of options from which to choose. We want their space to reflect their personality and to suit their lifestyles."

Secrets to Our Success

Don't resist change. Early on, Art and Sarah advertised with Home Advisor. That helped them initially get their name out there. But they've since moved away from it, instead focusing on generating more traffic to their own website.

Read to learn about business. The couple recommends *Profit First* *for Contractors* and *Lobster on a Cheese Plate*, for example, as quick marketing guides for small businesses. Craftsmen limit themselves by not focusing on their own growth in understanding what it means to own a successful business.

Find your niche. "We've narrowed our focus down to doing finish work," explained Art. "We specialize in built-in, custom storage solutions, for example, adding bookshelves to an office, cabinets to a mudroom, or sporting-equipment cubbies in a garage." It's important to focus your efforts where they will be most beneficial for growth.

Nurture relationships. "We have many returning customers, and we love them," Sarah said. "Families hire us for one project in one room, and then they often will come back months or years later to do another project in another room, then another. They know that we are not going to pressure them with upsells, and we are always responsive and available to help them plan for projects *when they are ready.*"

Strategize together. "Art and I constantly discuss strategic planning for our business," Sarah said. "Because we were really good friends long before we started AWM Carpentry, we have a strong friendship in addition to being married business partners. We fall back on our friendship a lot. We know when one of us is stressed and when one of us is excited and wants to share. We understand and complement each other well."

As the pair plans for their bright future, they are creating systems to allow for growth. "We envision bigger things," Art said. "We are interested in growing. We want this company to be the first thing that pops into people's heads when they think of customizing their homes."

For More Information

- AWMCarpentry.com

- 610-390-3341

- office@awmcarpentry.com

- 303 Blue Mountain Drive, Walnutport, PA 18088

- Services offered: Custom trim, custom woodwork, and stairs and railings

1COR6:19 FITNESS

We Tend to Our Clients' Spirit. Soul. Body.

In 2015, Niki Swasey was having some health challenges and needed surgery. She wanted to get into better shape, knowing that the stronger she went into surgery, the stronger she would come out. Niki had met Devon Swasey at Life Church in Macungie and knew he was a personal fitness trainer.

The pair met at Rodale Park for a personal training assessment. Devon prepared a personalized fitness program for Niki to attain her goals. After several weeks of training, people in their church started to notice Niki's physical transformation. Impressed by Niki's success and Devon's training program, other church members sought his training.

Shortly after, the church held a health seminar about Faith and Fitness. Devon and Niki were asked to co-facilitate a Bible Study that paralleled the vision of the health seminar, solidifying their reputations as the faces of fitness within the church.

Over the next few months, Devon, who had a firm foundation in fitness training—including certifications in personal training, strength and conditioning, running, and cardio boxing—saw his personal training business flourish. He knew that Niki had tremendous experience working with the body and also in business, so he asked if she could help him train. Back then, they worked with their clients at parks, churches, and open gyms. A dream began to form in their minds though, to have their own location.

During their Bible Study, a Bible verse that continued to weave in and out of conversation resonated with them: 1 Corinthians 6:19: Do you not know that your bodies are the temples of the Holy Spirit, who is in you, whom you have received from God? You are not your own.

"The meaning of that verse spoke to us," said Niki, who also has certifications in personal training, strength and conditioning and nutrition, plus a license in massage therapy, along with a background in rehabilitation.

"It's so important to honor your body by exercising well, eating healthy foods, seeing and hearing positive messages, understanding that our body belongs to God," Niki said. "During our early conversations about opening our own

At right: Devon and Niki Swasey, Owners of 1COR6:19 FITNESS

Devon Swasey, Co-Owner of 1COR6:19 FITNESS

fitness center, this became much more than a business. It became a ministry."

"We decided to nickname it '1COR' as a reference to the book of the Bible but also because of the importance of training your body's core," Devon explained. "Our philosophy is that the CORe of the body is the muscles from your shoulders to your knees, front side and back side. That's a broader definition than most people have. We strengthen our clients' bodies by starting with CORe Strengthening."

In 2016, Devon and Niki started their limited liability corporation. "There's never a right financial state to take a leap like this," Niki said. "It's scary. But we were ready to take that leap of faith."

With their business founded, Devon and Niki started searching for their fitness studio location. They came close to leasing a property in a basement in Emmaus when a friend called to tell them about a property becoming available in Breinigsville. The friend had seen people moving gym equipment out of it—certainly a promising sign. That night, Devon and Niki went to see it and prayerfully realized, "It's perfect. It's exactly what we need."

The doors to 1COR opened at 7 am on July 17, 2017, auspicious because seven is known as the number of completion. The gym opened with pieced-together equipment, including their own gym equipment moved from their garages. Niki placed her mountain bike atop a stand to make a stationary bike. At first, they used an expandable folder to hold cash—until clients gifted them a cash box.

"We come from really humble beginnings," Niki said. "When you're starting out, fancy things do not matter."

The fitness studio began to grow. At the end of the day, regardless of the equipment, the critical piece of training is the *trainer*.

"Our trainers will remain positive and uplifting, demanding yet encouraging, all with our client's best interests in mind," Niki said. "We're equipped with experience, determined to support you in attaining your goals, and passionate about your long-term success."

1COR6:19 FITNESS offers personal training a la carte and also in packages, which lowers the per-session rate, making training more affordable. Bundles that offer multiple services to enhance an overall health/wellness program are also available.

As their relationship grew from business to personal, Devon and Niki were planning to get married in Devon's homeland, Jamaica, West Indies, in 2020. They went on their second missions trip in December 2019 to Matehuala, Mexico, in support of a ministry near and dear to their hearts. On that trip, Devon received a very strong feeling that they were meant to be married then and there, not to wait until 2020 in Jamaica.

Niki was hesitant, but sought God's plan through prayer, and heard Him say, "Now is the time."

At astonishing speed, the pastors, other missionaries, and their friends in Mexico organized a wedding, complete with a dress for Niki, clothes for Devon, beautiful floral arrangements, live acoustic guitar and harmonious Spanish singing. Their Holy Spirit led Mexican wedding was more than perfect, ending with a reception full of love and Mexican treats. The pair then had their official legal wedding back home, at their gym.

Ironically, they wouldn't have been able to take their Jamaican honeymoon-wedding in 2020 anyway. Their original wedding date was at the height of what turned out to be the Covid-19 pandemic.

"A few months after we got home from Mexico, the world shut down," Niki said. "Our Jamaican wedding wouldn't have happened."

Niki Swasey, Co-Owner of 1COR6:19 FITNESS

Although the pandemic didn't affect their wedding, it *did* impact their business. Fortunately in January 2020, the fitness studio had implemented a brand-new nutrition program, which helped them keep their studio doors open. Niki customizes meal plans according to each person's weight loss and fitness goals. With Niki's guidance, clients get their bodies to a place of balance by eating whole, natural foods.

"It's most effective when people combine our nutrition program with regular workouts," Niki said. "I tell my clients 'not to worry about that number on the scale.' So many people get so hung up on that."

Devon and Niki have not given up faith, knowing the cards were stacked against them during Covid. A large percentage of small fitness studios have gone out of business post-Covid, but by the grace of God and the support of their members, 1COR is still open to help change lives through overall wellness.

"We have a heart for helping people," Niki said. During the pandemic, they offered their classes over zoom at no charge or for a donation. As part of their ministry, they tithe sessions each month to those in need, considering it a blessing, as they follow the biblical principle of sowing seeds.

In early 2021, the couple's beautiful miracle baby was born. "I struggled post-partum getting back into a routine and fitness regimen," Niki said. "I started to research metabolic hormone balancing to help myself through challenging hormonal changes. Through my research and implementation of a specific nutrition and workout regimen, I ended up creating a program for women of all ages and stages of life that we are rolling out in 2024!"

Over the past few years, their fitness studio has evolved and grown into an overall wellness center.

"We pride ourselves on the one foundational aspect of the body in which we focus: the CORe," Niki said. "As faith is the foundation to our lives, the CORe is the foundation to strengthening the body. Without a foundation, how can we build anything? We strive to make health and wellness a priority in the lives of God's children. Our passion is helping others realize their full potential and achievements within their fitness goals and to do so exceedingly."

Today, the studio offers many classes for every level. No matter the class size, everyone gets the individual attention they need. They also have a sauna; including infrared therapy and red light therapy, which is wonderful for muscle recovery and soreness and for increasing collagen production; and halotherapy, which is medical-grade salt that is milled very finely for inhalation but it is also absorbed through the skin. It's especially beneficial for the prevention of viral and bacterial infections but also aids in healing respiratory illnesses.

Everyone is welcome to train and heal at 1COR6:19 FITNESS. "Some people come to us very defeated," Niki said. "We stand alongside our clients in fitness and in life. We pray with them and for them. We've had people pray aloud for the first time within these walls."

"When people come here, they often say, 'There's a different energy in this place,'" Devon said. "We are passionate about health and wellness. Our purpose is to help anyone and everyone we can live a healthier life. For us, instilling healthy lifestyle changes in every person we encounter is a moral responsibility. Our clients love being encouraged by one another and we truly have become a family. A sense of community has been established and this is so important in today's world. To witness the encouragement and motivation our clients give one another is such a blessing. They want to succeed for themselves and for each other!"

Secrets to Our Success

Trust in a higher power. "We put God first," Devon said. "Everything stems from His grace and our belief and trust in Him."

Do what you love. "It's never arduous to work alongside Devon all day then go home and be together all night," Niki said. "Our work is fun. It's the work that we've been called to do, and it's our passion in life. Because of that, coming into this gym every morning is not a chore. It's not work."

Stay in your own lane. "Niki is good at what she does, and I'm good at what I do, and we each stay in our own lane," Devon said.

"Our strengths and weaknesses complement each other," Niki added. "We never had to have a conversation to divide up tasks. It's just understood. Things that I don't enjoy doing, he naturally does and vice versa."

"And she keeps me in line," Devon joked.

Devon and Niki would like to thank all of their past and current clients for their love, support, prayers and belief in their mission. "Our clients mean the world to us, they have brought 1COR together as a community and gym family," Niki stated. "At 1COR we are stronger together," Devon added, "LET'S GET IT DID"!

For more information

- www.1cor619fit.com

- 610-241-7331

- 1cor619fit@gmail.com

- 1044 Trexlertown Road, Suite 108, Breinigsville, PA 18031

- Services offered: Personal training, semi-private training, fitness classes, youth fitness program, cardio-boxing, halotherapy, infrared therapy, red light therapy, and nutrition

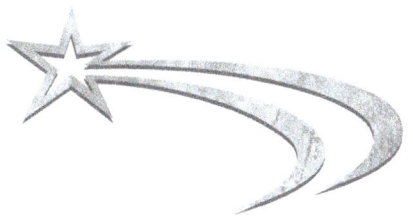

Audra Frank Associates, AFA Renovate, and Audra's Finishes and Design

We are a Powerhouse Renovator,
Redesigning the Homes of A-List Celebrities and Everyday People

Audra Carbaugh couldn't wait to move to New York City in the 1970s. Two of her first jobs in the city were painting and tending bar. She and a bunch of her fellow waitresses formed a painting company. The small company wasn't making enough money, so Audra got a job as a salesperson for a paint store in the Forest Hills neighborhood of Queens. She was then transferred to the company's store on 72nd Street at Janovic Plaza. That's where she earned her painting chops—and met her future husband, David Frank, who was the manager there.

"I didn't like him at first," she laughed. "But one thing led to another, and after some time we became an item."

The couple later married and took over what was left of David's family painting business in the Chelsea neighborhood of New York City.

"The early 1980s was a scary time in that neighborhood," Audra remembered. "There were junkies everywhere. I'd take the cash and checks from the day's sales in an old bank envelope and walk as fast as I could to the drop box, the whole time thinking, someone is going to hit me over the head and grab this money!"

Because of Audra's background as a painter and the fact that the paint store had a reputation of being quite prestigious, top people from all over the city would come to have their paint colors matched.

Besides painting, Audra began calling on customers and designers because she saw how receptive they were to her in the store. "That worked out well for me because once I got out of the paint store, I had the opportunity to take over my father-in-law's business."

At left: Audra Frank, Owner of Audra Frank Associates

"My father-in-law was an incredible painter and also an incredible teacher," Audra said.

"I learned so much just from being with him. I would change from my dress from seeing clients and put my painter's pants on and go to Broadway between 57th and 58th. We did a lot of work for famous people in there, including for MTV networks, Newsweek, and KMP Partners."

In 1984, David's father-in-law sold David and Audra the business. They continued to be very successful because they did things the old-fashioned way.

"My husband was an incredible job estimator, and his pricing was always very fair,"

Audra said. "We did high-quality work in a timely fashion. In New York, there's a Franklin Report, where customers rate companies on a five-star scale. We routinely got 4.5 stars, and people always had complimentary things to say about us."

At that time, Audra and David joined an organization called PDCA, the Painting and Decorating Contractors of America. Audra served as its president on an eight-state council from New Jersey to the Carolinas. "I learned a lot from taking classes through PDCA about working on my business as opposed to in my business," she said.

In the late 1980s, Audra and David incorporated their business, naming the company Audra Ingram Inc. Ingram was her husband's middle name.

Although the family business was still going strong, much had changed in the painting industry in the New York/New Jersey area. "The bidding was ridiculous," Audra said. "I'm not sure how businesses were doing the work for the money they bid in New York and New Jersey in the 1980s."

The last straw came one morning when Audra saw her son riding a skateboard, hanging onto the back of a box truck careening down 2nd Avenue. "We're moving," she told her husband.

In 1983, David and Audra moved to Scotch Plains, then to Warren, New Jersey.

Over the next few decades, Audra and David built their north Jersey painting and wallcoverings business into a thriving enterprise with a client list that included the homes of major sports figures like New York Jets players, famous musicians such as Paul Simon and Sting, and movie stars like Meryl Streep and Olympia Dukakis. Their commercial business was equally successful, with accounts like MTV, Comedy Central, and Viacom.

But sadly, after daily exposure to paint fumes for all those years, David developed brain cancer. It took his life in 2005.

In David's honor, Audra created a scholarship fund. For several years,

An Audra Frank Associates' kitchen renovation in progress

one promising high school student from New Jersey was chosen to be the recipient.

After David's passing, "green" took on a new meaning for Audra. Now it meant the life or death of people you love. She decided to go on providing the same services as before, but with a new purpose: Promoting healthy indoor air quality. Because of David's battle with brain cancer, Audra's company underwent a major shift. She is now a contractor on a mission to use green products and provide green installations.

Audra kept working under the name Audra Frank Painting name until 2019. "I decided not to do it anymore," she said. "I was getting up at 5:30 every

St. Philip and St. James Catholic Church, Phillipsburg, New Jersey

day, usually the first person on site, making all the decisions, and being the quality-control person."

Secrets to Our Success

Go for quality consistently. Over the past several years, Audra has combed the marketplace for contracting products that do not release volatile organic compounds (VOCs) into the air. She knows which wallpaper glues, removers, soaps, and finishes you can use and still keep your surroundings safe. She uses only no-or low-VOC paints. Her wallpapers have no or little PVCs. Her cleaning products, removers, and adhesives are all environmentally friendly.

Tailor to meet customers' needs. Customers can make use of Audra's knowledge and experience in two ways: Contractors, architects, and designers can bring Audra in during the early stages of their projects to guarantee that they will deliver the highest level of environmentally friendly finished product. She makes sure the projects start green and stay green.

And homeowners can hire Audra Frank Associates to manage projects, such as interior or exterior painting, wallpaper hanging, decorative painting, stucco, faux finishes, and specialty wall coverings.

Know and value your community. In 2006, Audra moved once more, this time to Stewartsville, New Jersey.

"I feel very safe here," she said. I've come home after a long day at work, put on the TV, grabbed dinner, gone upstairs to sleep, and the next morning realized the keys were in the door all night long!"

Restoration of a landmark building in New York City

Today, Audra belongs to the Easton Chamber of Commerce, the Rotary Club, and a dining club called the Pomfret Club. Her son, Duston, doesn't want to be a part of the family business. He went to college and is a successful project manager for a large display company in Las Vegas.

In addition, Audra recently completed Green Build Science Certification Training. Today, she is focused on civic organizations and how she can help our community.

For More Information

 Eco-friendly Installations and Products

■ www.AudraFrankAssociates.com

■ 908-872-6112

■ afarenovate@gmail.com

■ Services offered: Eco-friendly commercial and residential painting and wall coverings

CarePatrol

Our Family Helps Families Choose the Right Senior Care Option

In 2014, Mary Ann Pickell was looking for a new opportunity to use her marketing and sales talent and experience. She was hired by the owner of the local CarePatrol franchise, which spans Lehigh, Northampton, and Upper Bucks counties, as the marketing director.

Founded by medical social worker Chuck Bongiovanni after he observed the trauma of a family member whose loved one was placed in the wrong type of facility, the company had been operating for about twenty years when Mary Ann joined CarePatrol. Mary Ann was drawn to the company because of its immense heart for helping seniors, which is its mission, immortalized by its purple, blue, and green heart-shaped logo.

"I've always loved older adults because in my lifetime most of my relatives were older," Mary Ann said. "I didn't have a lot of young relatives, so I think I had a predisposition to enjoy the company of my family's elders."

As part of her new role, Mary Ann became a CSA (Certified Senior Advisor). Through a series of courses, she learned how to guide older adults in their transition to the next stage of their lives. Her work for each of the hundreds of families she has helped includes navigating a web of health, financial, and family issues.

Often, families reach out to CarePatrol in crisis—an older adult has an illness or an injury that is forcing a change. Maybe the senior is no longer safe living at home alone, or perhaps the older adult is about to be released from a hospital. The seniors need help, now—and so does his or her family!

With dozens of senior care communities in the greater Lehigh Valley and Upper Bucks area from which to choose, deciding where to place a senior loved one would be challenging under normal circumstances. But it's nearly impossible to make a smart choice around this under pressure.

That's often when families reach out to CarePatrol—for their education and advocation helping the older adult transition to a new, better living situation.

At right: Front: Niki Alban and Carol Frawley. Back: Mary Ann Pickell, partner; Robert Pickell, partner; and Chloe Pickell, partner

"Ideally, people would think ahead and have a plan in mind. Because surprise! We are all aging!"—Robert Pickell

Over Mary Ann's first few years at CarePatrol, her responsibilities grew as she became the local CarePatrol franchisee's indispensable righthand. Little did she know, but Mary Ann was being immersed in her next opportunity. In 2019, the franchise owner wanted to sell the franchise. She approached Mary Ann and her husband, Robert, with the idea, and they decided to buy it.

"I loved what I was doing," Mary Ann said. "I didn't want to let the opportunity to buy the franchise pass me by."

The couple worked with the franchisee and corporate headquarters to purchase the local franchise. Mary Ann and Robert along with their financial partners, Charles and Carol Mest, bought the franchise in January of 2019. Since then, they have grown from a husband-and-wife team to adding a virtual assistant; Director of Community Relations, Carol Frawley; and a second Certified Senior Advisor, Niki Alban. Most recently, they added their daughter, Chloe Pickell, came on as their Director of Operations.

"My entire team is family to me. They are amazing," Mary Ann said. "Our daughter, Chloe, now does so much for our business, including new client intakes, follow-up calls, liaison with our communities, licensure verification, and all day-to-day operations to keep our staff informed and the office running smoothly."

The close-knit CarePatrol team works together to help hundreds of local families. This past year alone, the team helped place more than 250 seniors.

Over the years, just as Mary Ann and Bob's CarePatrol franchise has grown, CarePatrol has also grown nationally. Today, they are the nation's largest and most trusted senior living placement organization, with more than 170 local franchises throughout the country.

What has also grown is the variety and breadth of the senior communities that CarePatrol of the Lehigh Valley & Upper Bucks assists its clients in transitioning to.

"We work with over 100 care providers ," Mary Ann said. "We have vetted them all, and we routinely check their licensure."

Even more astonishing than the depth of the CarePatrol knowledge is the speed with which the CarePatrol team is able to match clients with the right

The CarePatrol Team celebrating after achieving a record-breaking month of assisting families in the Lehigh Valley and Upper Bucks region

senior community fit. When a family reaches out to CarePatrol, they ask questions about their loved one's health, home situation, finances and social needs. CarePatrol can also help the family if they need referrals to other experts, such as nonmedical home care, elder law attorneys, movers, or realtors. "We are very connected to all of these resources to help close that circle," Mary Ann said

One of their Certified Senior Advisors then personally consults with the client and his or her family. They then recommend two or three appropriate locations—out of the many they work with. Tours are arranged for the family, the CSA accompanies them so they can educate and advocate throughout the process.

"Once we understand what the older adult's care needs are, we are able to get a clear picture of which community would be the best fit for that senior," Mary Ann said.

But it's not just the client that CarePatrol is caring for—it's the whole family.

"Our client is the entire family," Mary Ann said. "As much as it's the older adult we are looking for care locations for, really we're bringing the family together to ascertain what their needs are."

"There's a lot of denial with all of us. It's hard to admit that we are getting older. But we have to think, what would I want? Then let your family know. Especially when people have multiple children, it can get complicated quickly. It's a heavy weight when a child has to make those decisions for his or her parent. We are here to help. We understand." —Mary Ann Pickell

But what is the most surprising part of this entire process is that this invaluable service is offered *free* to the older adults and their families. Care Patrol is paid by their pre-vetted senior care providers.

"I love what I do every day," Mary Ann said. "It's an honor to help families; I get as much out of helping them as they get out of being helped. What we hear most from people after we've helped them is, 'I feel so much better now that I've spoken with you.'"

And that feeling is not only free—it's priceless.

Secrets to Our Success

Play to your strengths. Collaborating with family works out beautifully for the Pickells. "Mary Ann is the face of our business," Bob said. "I handle the finances and other backend tasks so she doesn't have to worry about those things. That frees Mary Ann up to focus on being our company's heart and soul, focusing on the families."

Carve out private workspaces. Mary Ann and Bob run their business from their home and the entire CarePatrol team work virtually.

"We each have our own workspace," Mary Ann said. "I need to be on the phone all of the time and be able to talk freely with our clients, families, and communities, while Bob needs quiet so he can focus on finances and details. So, we each have our own office, and we come together to meet whenever we need to. After the workday, there might be some banter over dinner. But after that, we drop the shop talk."

Align with others. Mary Ann and Bob are part of a network of CarePatrol franchisees. "We work hand in hand with the other office so we can help families who live in different states," Mary Ann explained. "For instance, if a client is here in the Lehigh Valley but their family is in New Jersey and they want to relocate her there, we would do intake, then share that information with the New Jersey office, who would help the family find the right senior care solution."

"While we know the communities here in the Lehigh Valley, the New Jersey CarePatrol team members know their local communities," added Bob. "We rely on working with our partner offices to be better together."

Plan ahead. Most people are busy living their lives, not thinking ahead to which senior living community to move to someday.

"Ideally, people would think ahead and have a plan in mind," Bob said. "Because surprise! We are all aging!"

"There's a lot of denial with all of us," Mary Ann said. "It's hard to admit that we are getting older. But we have to think, what would I want? Then let your family know. Especially when people have multiple children, it can get complicated quickly. It's a heavy weight when a child has to make those decisions for his or her parent. We are here to help. We understand."

For More Information

- www.lehighvalley.carepatrol.com

- 610-509-0445

- mpickell@carepatrol.com

- PO Box 397, Center Valley, PA 18034

- Services offered: CarePatrol consults, advocates, and partners with families to find the right senior care solution for their loved one, including assisted living, independent living, memory care, in-home care, and more.

Redbox+ Dumpsters and Fish Window Cleaning

Our Family Takes on Tough Tasks

David Galkin was born in Ukraine and moved to Brooklyn, New York, at the age of three. Stephanie Zhang was born in China and moved to Philadelphia at 17. They met while they were in college—at the University of Massachusetts Amherst and Penn State University, respectively. David majored in philosophy; Stephanie in finance. After graduation, they decided to start a business together.

"What you hear is that starting a business is wonderful and full of rainbows and unns," David said. "That seemed like the perfect path for us."

The couple started to research owning a business and stumbled upon the idea of buying a franchise.

"We figured that's a good idea—why reinvent the wheel when you could buy one instead," David said. "We started working with a franchise consultant who gave us a list of 90 franchise concepts. Most people don't realize how many familiar businesses are actually franchises. With his help, we whittled that list down to two."

"We decided to buy a franchise rather than starting a business from scratch because a franchise has already been created. We knew we could hop on that and be taught how to run it," Stephanie added.

The pair decided to invest in an established franchise called Fish Window Cleaning.

"We were thinking ahead to having children, and we knew it was important to us to be with our kids once they were born," Stephanie said. "There are no window-cleaning emergencies at 2 am; it's a Monday through Friday, 9-to-5 type of business, so we figured it would be an excellent choice for a couple raising a family."

Fish Window Cleaning was founded in 1978. The founder chose its name

At left: David Galkin and Stephanie Zhang, Owners of Redbox+ Dumpsters

"What you hear is that starting a business is wonderful and full of rainbows and unicorns. That seemed like the perfect path for us."

—David Galkin

because the four-letter-word is easy to remember and because of that old adage about teaching a man to fish.

David and Stephanie invested all of their savings into their fledgling franchise, which they based in Allentown. Their plan was for Stephanie to leave her full-time job right away, with David following in her footsteps three or four months later.

"We wanted to get our Fish Window Cleaning franchise up and running as quickly as we could," David said. "Then we figured Stephanie could go back to her old job for the benefits and steady paycheck for as long as necessary."

The new franchise grew even more quickly than they expected. "I think it was because we were committed 120 percent," David said. "We were all hands on deck."

In the beginning, both David and Stephanie cleaned windows. Their clients were—and still are—about three-quarters commercial, such as restaurants, office buildings, and car dealerships—the types of places that really need clean windows!

Growth is rarely linear, though, and so Fish grew in fits and starts. "Sometimes we'd have too much work; other times we'd have too little," Stephanie said. "It's a chicken-or-the-egg situation: When do you have enough work to hire someone? And if you hire them, will you still have enough income to support yourself?"

Today, the company has 12 technicians, an office manager, and an operations manager. Out of 250 locations nationwide, their franchise is in the top 10, head-to head with much bigger markets such as Houston, Boston, and Los Angeles.

Having had such success with the Fish Window Cleaning Franchise, David and Stephanie began thinking maybe a second franchise would produce twice as good—maybe even exponential—results.

"We decided to get a second franchise because we like the franchise model," David said. "I've learned that I'm great at taking something that already exists and tweaking it, molding it to make it better. Turns out, creating something from scratch isn't my strong suit," he adds.

"We bought our redbox+ Dumpsters franchise in 2021," David said. "Fish was going so well it was on autopilot. My operations manager was running it, and we got bored, so we started looking at opening something else."

The pair chose redbox+ Dumpsters after doing a lot of research. The redbox+ Dumpster is a patented design that comes with a port-a-potty. Usually people have to make two phone calls to get a Dumpster and a port-a-potty, but with redbox+ Dumpsters they get both with just one call.

The redbox+ Dumpsters franchise is part of Belfor Franchise Group and is headquartered in Ann Arbor, Michigan, and David and Stephanie's location is in Easton. About three-quarters of their clients are contractors, with only one-quarter homeowners, usually people cleaning out their garage or basement. Their franchise has grown really fast, and they already have six trucks, six team members to drive them, an office manager, and 120 Dumpsters.

"We have some synergy between the two companies," David said. "We learned a lot running Fish Window Cleaning that we carried over to redbox+ Dumpsters."

Redbox+ Dumpsters at work

"If David is strong on one side of a decision, and I'm strong on the other, we work together to try to find a way to make both work. We've taken personality tests that helped us to better understand our styles. For example, David is a 'visionary,' and I'm an 'integrator.' We try to play to our strengths. I own what I'm good at."

—Stephanie Galkin

For example, when David and Stephanie opened their Fish Window Cleaning franchise, they were advised to start with door-to-door marketing—going to businesses, stores, restaurants, and car dealerships. They did that for almost a year until they had built up a strong client base. They used the same approach with redbox+ Dumpsters, although less literally door-to-door since that was during the COVID-19 pandemic.

Fortunately, the huge Dumpsters with "redbox+" in big letters on the sides work like billboards that speak for themselves.

"At this point, we have more than 120 of them in the Lehigh Valley," David said. "They're everywhere."

Today, the company is a family affair. Even their young children pitch in.

"We bring them out to the trucks, and they'll help detail them, cleaning and vacuuming the inside," Stephanie said.

And all that hard work from the oldest to the youngest really pays off: Theirs is the number one franchise out of 85 in the country, and this year they won Franchise of the Year for redbox+ Dumpsters.

David and Stephanie continue to set lofty goals for their businesses. "We hope to be able to retire when our kids go to college."

Secrets to Our Success

Separate personal and work life. "This is a challenge because that's all we do," said Stephanie. "I think sometimes we need to set boundaries, for example, not talking about business at dinner, but that's harder than you think. It requires a lot of discipline to try to separate your duties and also draw the same line between your business and your personal life."

Try to strike a compromise. "If David is strong on one side of a decision, and I'm strong on the other, we work together to try to find a way to make both work," Stephanie said. "We've taken personality tests that helped us to better understand our styles. For example, David is a "visionary," and I'm an "integrator." We try to play to our strengths. I own what I'm good at."

For instance, they had to decide whether to start their franchise with one truck or two. David wanted to start with two; Stephanie wished to be more conservative at one. They started with one, and it went well, so within three months they were able to buy the second truck.

Consider all sides before you invest. David and Stephanie warn that anyone who thinks the franchise journey is simply about following directions is mistaken.

"You see more and more franchise concepts now," David said. "A lot of people are trying to franchise their businesses—not always for good reasons. Just because you invest in a franchise doesn't mean it's going to be easier than starting your own independent business. It just shortens the tunnel to get from beginning to profitable. You still have to go through the tunnel."

"Yes, it shortens it maybe, but it's still a lot of hard work," Stephanie agreed. "A lot of people think when you buy a franchise, everything will be handed to you on a silver platter. That's not true. There's still a lot of hard work."

Don't expect the franchisor to do all the heavy lifting. "Starting a franchise isn't always about following the recipe. You have to customize and personalize it to help your customers achieve their goals."

For More Information

- www.redboxplus.com/lehighvalley
- 484-640-5517
- officelehigh@redboxplus.com
- 6034 Hamilton Blvd., Suite 119, Allentown, PA 18106
- Services offered: Dumpster rentals

Carl Volkman and Sons

We Keep Families Comfortable

As a young boy growing up in New York City, Carl Volkman loved tinkering around with his grandfather, a retired NYPD lieutenant.

"I was always helping him with projects," Carl remembered. "He had the mechanical ability to fix anything for anyone. He could do many tasks where most people would have no clue where to even begin. We were like farmers: We did everything. We fixed everything."

Time spent by his grandfather's side proved to be a thorough education in using tools and the fundamentals of understanding how things work—and how to repair them.

When Carl was fresh out of high school—just 18 years old—his first job was installing spray booth and dust-collection systems. He made just $7.20 per hour.

"It was okay for a first job—interesting but not satisfying," Carl said. "Until one day, we did an air-conditioning job. I saw a much clearer connection in that work to helping people. I was hooked."

Carl's company had been hired to install an AC system in the break room of a large warehouse for its employees.

"The AC work was more interesting because it was much more complicated. Even more valuable was the sense of accomplishment I had after finishing. When the AC unit was installed, we literally flipped the switch and the employees all cheered because they were so happy! They now got to take a lunch break and cool off instead of sweating all day. That's when I realized this is what I want to do with my life."

Carl worked at that company for a year, soaking up as much information about the HVAC field as he could. He was promoted to running a mainly Spanish-speaking crew. Even though Carl didn't speak much Spanish, he did a good job to mediate between the clients and crew. When he asked for a raise, his boss offered him a measly 15 cents an hour.

At right: Carl "el heffe" Volkman

"Not having heat in the winter or air-conditioning in the summer can be a life-threatening emergency. If the temperature is in the 20s or below, pipes can freeze, causing flooding, which wreaks the same amount of damage as a fire."

—Carl Volkman

"I was so insulted I left the company!" Carl said.

So he hit the streets of New York, applying to HVAC companies all over the city. It wasn't long before he had a new, better-paying job. Realizing there was more to be gained as a union worker, Carl joined HVAC union UA Local 638 and worked steadily for the next 10 years, mainly on high-rise buildings.

Fortunately, Carl isn't afraid of heights because a lot of the work was high off the ground—like 107 floors high!

"I saw some pretty shady stuff," Carl laughed. "But most of it was safe, and we usually had phenomenal views of the city!"

He recalled working one job on the 30th floor of a building with only a rope tied around his worker's waist! For another job, the men worked on the 107th floor of the Empire State Building—three floors above the observation deck, so they could look over the edge and see the tourists below—and the whole city stretched out before them. Not for the faint of heart!

"I never thought about the danger when I was young," Carl said.

Shortly into his HVAC career, Carl realized the value of his work. The company was often hired for critical jobs—like keeping the AC units humming in data centers. Once, they worked for a company that records all of the Wall Street data.

"They looked like sets in the Matrix—huge rooms of servers," Carl said. "If those servers ever go down, the companies would lose millions of dollars. In fact, for those companies, keeping those computers cool was prioritized over keeping their *employees* cool!"

Speaking of computers, over Carl's long career, he's seen vast, dramatic changes in HVAC technology.

"When I first started in the field in 1999, there were basic control boards, but they controlled a lot less. Now they control everything," Carl explained.

To keep up, Carl and other HVAC experts attend classes for the equipment they install and service. The types of equipment varies greatly—everything from AC for hay driers to MRI equipment.

After a decade in NYC, Carl started thinking about buying a home. He decided to move to Hellertown in 2011. His plan was to commute into the city each day! That idea quickly went out the window when his company refused to allow him to drive the company van across state lines!

So Carl did a quick pivot. He found a job for an HVAC company in Exton, Pennsylvania, mainly doing commercial work. Always eager to learn more, he started some side hustles. He'd work in Exton from 8 am to 4:30 pm, then come home and work until 2 am!

Pretty soon, the work and income from Carl's side hustle overtook his day job. In September 2015, he opened his business. Because he had so much work, he established his LLC in 2017 and took the leap to focus on his own work full-time, quitting the day job.

Today, Carl's business is split about 75 percent residential and 25 percent commercial. His business grew quickly, and he hired another team member in 2017. Then he brought on a second in 2019. His oldest son, Joe, started working with him last year, running the duct-cleaning division. "He was one

Carl Volkman installing a minisplit system for his cousin Justin in New York, who was one of his first supporters in 2015 when he opened his company

Carl Volkman's youngest son, Lucas, posing with a ductless minisplit the company installed for a finished basement in 2017

of my best team members," Carl remembered. "We have a great mutual respect for each other, and I thoroughly enjoyed working with him." Now Joe is pursuing a health care career with Lehigh Valley Health Network.

But that wasn't the end of the "family" part of Carl's "family business."

Carl is also excited for his youngest son, Lucas, to become a team member when he graduates from high school in 2024.

"Plus, without the love and support of my wife, Toni, taking care of the household and helping me with important decisions, paying company bills, and helping with many special projects such as making company T-shirts, I wouldn't be able to keep up with everything," Carl said.

In 2021, Carl's brother-in-law, Vinny, began working with him in the duct-cleaning division. "Vinny is like a younger brother to me," Carl said fondly. "It's so easy working with him. I love being able to help my family, too. But really everyone who works for me is like my family."

Carl even treats his clients like they are family. "I want people to know they can trust us," he said. "An HVAC unit can be a major purchase, and it's a complex one. It's critical to be honest and do the right thing. Our goal is to make customers for life."

Secrets to Our Success

Know your client. A particular favorite type of client for Carl is elderly. "I never want to see them taken advantage of by unscrupulous companies," he said. "They have put in their time in life, worked hard. They deserve respect and to be properly taken care of."

He recalled a story where one cold Saturday winter evening, the furnace in a senior care home in Bethlehem went down. Twenty elderly residents had no heat, and they were in severe danger in the frigid temperatures. But because of their age and health conditions, the seniors were too fragile to be moved.

It wasn't possible to fix the furnace in the night, so Carl and his team went to Home Depot and bought every single space heater in stock. They set up temporary heaters in the care home, plus they had an employee monitoring the heaters to make sure they were operating safely! On Sunday morning, they ascertained that the boiler was broken and leaking. There was no fixing it; it needed to be replaced. So first thing Monday morning, Carl's team found one and installed it.

Take your work seriously. "Not having heat in the winter or air-conditioning in the summer can be a life-threatening emergency," Carl cautioned. "If the temperature is in the 20s or below, pipes can freeze, causing flooding which wreaks the same amount of damage as a fire."

Carl shared a story of a client who came home from vacation to see water raining down into his kitchen and living room. A pipe had broken on the third story because the furnace wasn't working and pipes froze.

Keep adapting. Having helped thousands of families and companies in the past, Carl looks eagerly forward to taking a different direction. "In the future, I see us transitioning more toward commercial work," he said. "We've been doing more ductless mini-splits, which are small AC units that can be installed almost anywhere. They are extremely versatile and can be integrated into a house or installed as a standalone heating and air-conditioning system in a shed, pole barn, basement, finished attic— anywhere you don't want to add ductwork."

For More Information

- www.CarlVolkmanSons.com

- 484-704-2275 (work) and 718-612-4639 (cell)

- carl72003@gmail.com

- 468 Maple Road, Hellertown, PA 18055

- Services offered: Residential and commercial heating and cooling

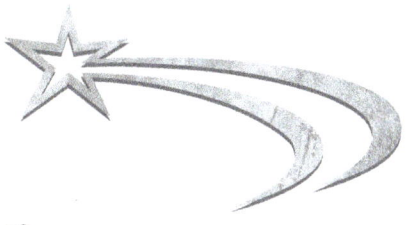

Dance with Kim

Our Family Changes Lives Through Dance

Kim Semmel started dancing when she was just four years old, taking ballet classes at the ballet theater in Hazleton.

"I was one of those little girls who hung onto my mom's legs and cried before every class," Kim remembered. It was a new experience, and I was a shy child.

Today, when children nervously come to their first classes, clinging to their moms' legs, Kim feels their emotions to her core. But she smiles and welcomes them to class, knowing how much dance will help improve their self-confidence, self-esteem, and lives.

When Kim was in elementary school, she began taking dance classes in a studio in Lansford. Rather than the discipline and structure of ballet classes, Kim studied tap, jazz, and baton classes.

"Ballet was more disciplined, and that wasn't the thing for me at that time," Kim said." I enjoyed the energy and pace of tap and jazz."

As a girl, Kim loved the friendships and camaraderie that dance had to offer, but even more she loved the excitement and performance opportunity at the end of each season—showcases, as she calls them—the costumes, makeup, and especially the opportunity to bring her family together. "I loved having the support of friends and family."

Dance became so integral to Kim's life that by junior high school her mom registered her for classes in Binghamton, New York. This was a three-hour drive after school. The programs were strict, but the results were well worth the dedication and work. At this point she already knew what she wanted to do with her life: become a director and choreographer of a dance studio. She began teaching privately in the living room of her home with just a handful of students who knew her and shared her love of dance.

When Kim graduated from high school in 1987, she went to a local bank and asked for a loan to purchase mirrors, a ballet barre, and a sound system. Despite

At left: Back: Dan Semmel, Mike Semmel, Donna Graver, and Harry Pry. Front: Zaviah Semmel, Kim Semmel, Brittany Semmel-Pry, and Evelyn Pry: the Dance with Kim team

Kim Semmel, Director and Owner of Dance with Kim, and Brittany Semmel-Pry, Co-Director of Dance with Kim, in 1998

the fact that she was only eighteen years old, the banker was impressed by Kim's confidence and business plan, and he gave her the $5,000 loan she needed.

"Looking back, I can hardly believe I had the courage to do that," she said. "But I didn't have anything to lose. I didn't have a spouse or children to care for, nor a car payment or mortgage to pay. I figured 'I'll just pay my rent, try it out, and see how it goes.'"

And it went really well. With that money, Kim opened a very small studio—only a little bigger than an office—on 1st Street in Lehighton. That first year, Kim had thirty students. After six months, Kim's studio had already grown enough to move across town to its current location at 248 South 4th Street. She rented that large building for a few years, then bought it.

Kim met her high school sweetheart, Mike, in 1985 and the two married in 1989. Their son, Dan, was born in 1991, and her daughter, Brittany, arrived in 1995. In 2000, the family moved into the apartment above the dance studio.

"It had been tough to maintain our home and the studio building across town," Kim explained. "So we sold our home and moved above the studio. That turned out to be a huge blessing because when my kids were little, my grandmother would come babysit them. Later, my kids would come home from school and go right upstairs while I taught classes downstairs. I knew where they were at all times."

Over the years, as the dance industry grew and evolved, so did Kim's studio. Today, she and her daughter welcome close to 300 students a week. To accommodate that growth, Kim recruited a former student, her daughter, husband, son, and mother to help in her multi-generational family business.

"Working with family is both rewarding and challenging," she said. "Like

"In a world where you can be anything, be kind."

with any team, you learn to work with each person's challenges and use each person's strengths. Finding a partner in life who supports my dreams has been a huge plus for me. My family is also completely supportive and all want the business to succeed. Organization and an open line of communication with our clients are very important to our success."

Today, Kim shares the title of dance studio director with her daughter, Brittany. Kim's husband, Mike, does the payroll and helps create the annual

Brittany Semmel-Pry, Co-Director of Dance with Kim and a graduate of the University of the Arts, doing a tilted Jete on Broad Street in Philadelphia in 2017

showcase program book and is in charge of ticket sales. Brittany, who majored in dance at the University of the Arts in Philadelphia, does much of the social media and marketing, directs the dance team students, does most of the choreography and all costuming. Brittany's interests dovetail nicely with Kim's because her favorite dance style is ballet. Son Dan supports as administrative assistant, helps with props at shows and assists where needed with other performances. Kim's mother has worked the front desk for many years, answering questions and helping students and parents alike.

Kim has two granddaughters, born in 2018 and 2021. Both girls enjoy their time at the studio and have already started making lifelong friendships.

The studio's curriculum has inspired confidence in thousands of students, placing students on countless local dance teams and in college programs. In addition to teaching ballet, tap, jazz, pointe, acrobatic arts, contemporary, and summer dance camps, the studio brings in guest teachers throughout the year from New York, New Jersey, and beyond. It also hosts an event called Dancer Mania, which is open to all students and to surrounding studios. A popular part of their program is competitive dance. The students travel to nearby competitions in Lancaster, King of Prussia, Philadelphia, and even into New Jersey.

While most of the students are girls, each year several boys take the opportunity to take classes as well. The school of dance also offers mini sessions for adults.

"Most adults are too busy to commit to a year-long class, but they can often fit in six weeks to eight weeks of a specialty class," Kim explained.

As Kim knows from her own dance experience, the ability dance has to boost confidence and self-esteem has the power to transform lives.

"Dance offers so many benefits to children and adults," Kim said. "It helps with mental and physical health, lasting friendships, social skills, time management, and more. Our kids' lives are so much more stressful now. But they can let that all go here and dance. It's valuable for their mental well-being. It also helps with their physical health. Our students value their time and work very hard in class"

"We work hard to nurture a family atmosphere here," she said. "When our students come to the studio, they can check their school or home troubles at the door. Our studio is a safe environment for them to express themselves through dance and often becomes a second home.

The family's state-of-the-art facility is impressive, too! It offers large observation windows and television monitors for parents to observe class and students' progress throughout the year. Suspended wood floors help reduce the risk of injury and prevent fatigue.

The studio works hard to make life easier for their students' busy parents. First, they are at a convenient location in Lehighton. Also, they afford parents the ability to schedule multiple classes at the same location and save travel time between activities. Their superb customer service means office staff is always available during class times to help with parents' questions and concerns.

Organization is key, and busy parents are updated with newsletters, social media posts, and text messages. Plus, the Dance with Kim studio website updates parents and students weekly about upcoming events.

All of that hard work has paid off. Over the years, Dance with Kim has taught tens of thousands of students. And Kim and her family don't plan to slow down anytime soon.

"My husband says, 'There's no way you're going to retire. You have too much fire in you,'" Kim said with a smile. "I hope in the future, that we continue to attract students to our facility for learning, friendship, and growth—in dance and also in growing as better humans and assets to our community."

Secrets to Our Success

Ease off the reins. "Most of the time, working with family is great," Kim enthused. "But sometimes we butt heads. When that happens, I suggest, 'Why don't we give your idea a try and see what happens.'" Sometimes the new idea is successful, and other times it's not. But either way, we gave it a try."

Give back when you are able. "Our family started a nonprofit organization, Dance with Kim for a Cause," one of my daughter's ideas," Kim said proudly. "Last year we donated $2,000 to local veterans organizations. Before that we gave $2,500 to nearby fire companies." The studio also participates in local charities and nonprofit organizations. We like for our students to give back to their community that gives so much to them."

For More Information

- www.dancewithkim.com

- 610-377-4884

- misskim@ptd.net

- 248 South 4th Street, Lehighton, PA 18235

- Services offered: Dance classes, including ballet, jazz, tap, pointe, contemporary, modern, and acrobatic arts

The Brothers That Just Do Gutters—Lehigh Valley

We Provide a Seamless Experience

Jimmy Olang grew up in a small village in Kenya called Oyugis, where he and his family farmed the land, raised goats and sheep, and collected water from the river. He lived with his grandmother until he was twelve years old, while his father worked toward a business degree in the United States.

Jimmy's local church hosted U.S. missionaries, and Ken Parsons, the founder of The Brothers That Just Do Gutters, was one of them. The two became fast friends.

"When Ken left, he told me he wanted me to work for him if I ever moved to America," Jimmy said.

In 2001, Jimmy moved to the Hudson Valley region in New York. Jimmy reconnected with Ken at church and was offered a job on the spot. Ladders, gutters, and work boots were new to him.

Jimmy's wife, Jessi, had grown up in the Lehigh Valley. She went to college to become a teacher, and she enjoyed her work teaching at Dieruff High School in Allentown. In 2009, looking to date, she signed up for a free trial on a Christian dating service. And that's where she met Jimmy.

"Jimmy teases me that I owe the company money for the subscription," Jessi said. The couple was engaged after three months, but the two dated long-distance for a year before they were married. Then Jessi moved from the Lehigh Valley to the Hudson Valley, and the couple bought their first home.

At the time, Jimmy was working two full-time jobs to make ends meet. He worked long days hanging gutters, sometimes until 9 or even 10 pm, then quickly shoveled down some supper before working overnight at a group home for mentally disabled people. Teaching jobs were scarce back then, so rather than Jessi looking for work, the Olangs decided to start their family.

Their older daughter was born in 2011, and when Jessi was pregnant with their older son, Jimmy lost his overnight job—the one that provided the young

At right: Jimmy and Jessi Olang, Owners of The Brothers That Just Do Gutters

The Olang family: Lucy, Lincoln, Jessi, Jimmy, Logan, and Leeland

family's health benefits.

"That was a huge wake-up call for us," Jessi remembered.

Jimmy's boss at The Brothers That Just Do Gutters helped the family out with a pay raise. But Jimmy was starting to think, *I'm not going to be able to climb up and down ladders forever.* "My jobs had provided me a safe haven and income, but I was tired of constantly working," Jimmy said.

He began to imagine what the next best step would be. At the time, The Brothers That Just Do Gutters was about to offer franchises of their business.

"When I learned of that opportunity, I thought, maybe this is what I was looking for—a life where I don't have to work 100 hours a week and be constantly tired and never home for my family," Jimmy said.

"We really prayed a lot, and we felt like we were being led to start the first official franchise with Brothers Gutters," Jessi added.

After weeks of tough—but smart—negotiating, Jimmy and Jessi became the first franchisees. The territory they purchased was carefully chosen: The Lehigh Valley.

"We were terrified," Jimmy said. "We didn't know the first thing about running a business. As it turned out, we were their prototype as there are now more than 130 Brothers Gutters franchises."

Opening their franchise in the Lehigh Valley paid off because Jessi had so many connections here. "We had so many people here rooting for us," Jimmy said. But still it was hard work with Jimmy working seventeen-hour days and Jessi helping and staying home with their children.

Originally, the plan was for Jessi to help with the business until the company got going, but a decade and a half later, she's still there. "We really fell in love with business ownership, which I never anticipated," she said. "We bought the franchise as a means to provide for our family. I never could have predicted how much we would love what we are doing."

The company began with just one truck, one apprentice, and a ten-by-ten-foot office. But Jimmy and Jessi always acted as if it was a multi-million-dollar company. And today it is. Their franchise has grown to seven trucks and twenty employees. They began with the Lehigh Valley territory, then they expanded into Berks County and more recently, into Bucks County as well.

The Brothers That Just Do Gutters-Lehigh Valley has grown at twice the rate of other franchises. Jessi credits Jimmy's drive for their growth.

"My motivation is driven by healthy fear," Jimmy said, laughing. "I've always worked hard. Nothing in my life was handed to me. I'm always running away from my fears and toward growth."

Today, The Brothers That Just Do Gutters franchisers look to Jessi and Jimmy as model franchisees. Jessi even coaches and mentors new franchisees.

"This franchise is truly a brotherhood," Jessi said. "If I go a week without talking with another franchisee, that's highly unusual. We reach out to each other with questions, ideas, and support."

Over the years, their family grew right along with their business. They have four children, and the number of family members working has grown, too. Jimmy's brother joined the company, and Jessi's dad works as their warehouse manager in Allentown. None of this happened by accident. The Olangs have been focused on growth since the beginning. Even the children have helped them paint walls and such.

"When we started our company, our goal was to build a business that impacted many, many people," Jimmy said. "We wanted to provide opportunities for as many people as possible. Launching our business has transformed our lives, and we make an effort to do the same for the people who work for us. Our employees have opportunities to be promoted and achieve success. One of our employees has been with us since our first month, and is doing very well."

"We attract great people who work with us for a long time," Jessi added. "In

"When I learned of the opportunity to invest in a Brothers That Just Do Gutters franchise, I thought, maybe this is what I was looking for—a life where I don't have to work 100 hours a week and be constantly tired and never home for my family."

—Jimmy Olang

Jimmy Olang and his dad, Boaz Olang, during treatment in 2023

our industry, which is plagued by high turnover, several of our installers, our sales rep, and our general manager have all been with us since 2018."

"We've created a successful, balanced life between working hard and having time for our family of four children," Jimmy said. "I never thought I'd be a business owner. My dream was to work hard and earn American dollars. But the day I set foot in this country, I had an incredible opportunity that, combined with hard work, helped me get to where I am today."

"Resilience is molded in the fires of adversity," Jimmy says, and 2023 proved to be so, both professionally and personally.

The hardest adversity was Jimmy's dad being diagnosed with pancreatic cancer in 2023. It devastated the family. Jimmy and his dad have always had a special relationship. Jimmy credits everything he is to his Uncle Zadock and Grandma (both of whom partly raised Jimmy and his siblings), his mom, and most of all, his dad, Boaz.

"Many people contributed to who I am today, and I'm eternally grateful. But no one had a bigger impact than my dad," Jimmy said. "He's my anchor! Just like his father and his father before, going back generations, our journey is never static. It is to keep moving. My dad's job is to keep the traditions alive, passing on the baton to the next generation of Olangs. His impact in my life is forever cemented in who I have become and will continue to become, shouldering the responsibility of emulating the perfect family man, visionary, dreamer, educator, and impact maker he always modeled for me. Generations of Olangs will remember and honor my father through the ages."

Looking toward the future, Jimmy and Jessi want to continue to expand their strong tradition of philanthropy. They work with and donate to charities and organizations, such as Duke Delights and the Love Ran Red Foundation.

"We are on a very successful trajectory," Jimmy said. "We will continue to do everything we can to have an impact on our communities, our employees, and their families," Jimmy said.

Secrets to Our Success

Work as a team. "Many small businesses have trouble growing because they're stuck in the day-to-day work of running the company," Jimmy said.

"As general manager and sales manager, Jessi has the ability to get a bird's-eye view of the company. Her seeing that bigger picture allowed us to make long-term plans for growth. She's also the brains of the operation. She is able to look at a situation, identify what needs to be done, and make it happen."

"We see this as a race-to-replace. My goal was to get out of the field and into the office. Grooming team members to replace us in leadership roles has helped us scale dramatically. The first move was hiring our back-office adminstrator. This freed both Jessi and me to look at the big picture rather than running the day-to-day operations."

"What makes us a great team is that Jimmy is more risk-taking and forward-thinking than I am," Jessi added. "He's always pushing us forward. If it wasn't for him, I'd be inclined to stay in my comfort zone, thinking, *I'm good right here.*"

The couple both stressed that they are not "yes men" to one another. "You can imagine what most of our fights are about," Jessi joked.

"I prefer to call them "acceleration arguments," Jimmy teased.

Surround yourself with positivity. "From the beginning, we surrounded ourselves with great people," Jessi said. "We found people who could cheer us on, but also people who could mentor us, and even people who could challenge us."

Have a clear vision. Each year since the Olangs started their company, they've created a vision statement. That has been key to their success. Those vision statements have always been focused on giving their customers the best experience possible and educating their employees. "We've always tried to keep going and growing, and we've lived up to that vision very well," Jessi said.

Offer superior customer service. The Brothers Gutters franchisor tagline is "Reinventing customer service." "That has been our focus," Jessi said," We want all our customers to have a superior experience. We don't just want them to have their gutters done. We want them to enjoy the process of having their gutters done."

"We want it to be seamless," Jimmy joked, like their seamless gutters.

For More Information

- www.BrothersGutters.com

- 610-285-7770

- Jimmy@BrothersGutters.com

- 1302 North 18th Street, Allentown, PA 18104

- Services offered: Just gutters!

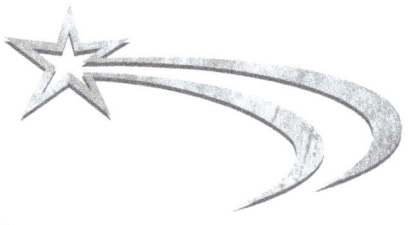

GuaranDeed Real Estate

We Bring People Home

"Real estate is in my blood," said Kiersten Vogt, sales agent at GuaranDeed Real Estate in Abington, Pennsylvania. "My mom was flipping houses before flipping was cool."

Kirsten's parents, Dennis and Cindy Vogt, bought their first home in a sheriff's sale in 1986. "They were bitten by the real estate bug," Kiersten joked. Cindy got her real estate broker's license and founded GuaranDeed Real Estate in 2014.

As Kiersten grew up, she watched her parents successfully buy and sell dozens of properties. Even though Kiersten knew she wanted to work in real estate, her parents "urged" her to go to college. She attended Penn State Main Campus, where she majored in business management.

"In the end, I'm glad my parents made me go," she said. "The lifelong friends I made were the best part of college."

Kiersten worked hard in college and graduated a semester early in 2009. She made great use of that bonus time, studying for and passing her real estate license. At that time, even though Kiersten was eager to join her parents' real estate business, her parents "urged" her to get another job. She was hired as a leasing consultant for Scully Company.

That work experience proved to be more beneficial to me than college, Kiersten said. She worked her way up the ranks to property manager, managing more than 200 rental units. Plus the company paid for her to attend classes on fair housing, leasing, and other related topics.

Around that time, Kiersten also began working with her parents, splitting the cost of properties 50/50. She was just twenty-three years old.

Then in 2012, Kiersten met her husband, Todd Dallas. He's a contractor with his own remodeling business, so together they became the property-flipping dream team.

"When I met Todd, I remember thinking, *This could work out really well*," Kersten said. "I love working with him. We make a really great team!"

At left: Kiersten Vogt and Todd Dallas, of GuaranDeed

In 2014, Kiersten officially joined GuaranDeed as a sales agent. She works as both a seller's agent and a buyer's agent.

"I love working with my mom," she said. "We've always gotten along very well, and we have a very close relationship. I can call her any time of the day, and I never feel like I'm bothering her. She gets just as excited about my deal as I do, and I love talking with her about our business."

Kiersten's sister, Kathryn, works in a related field. She's an underwriter for PNC bank; however she focuses on commercial lending, and GuaranDeed works mainly on residential properties.

The couple bought several properties and flipped them together. They bought their current home in 2020. "It was an auction, and we literally bid on our home standing on the front lawn," Kiersten remembered. "We've bought five properties at auctions. It's a good way to get great deals."

Today, the pair is finishing renovating their home. "Growing up, I learned a lot about renovations from my dad," Kiersten said. "Now, working with Todd, I've learned even more. He's a perfectionist. He always does things the right way. He doesn't cut corners—not even if a client asks him to."

That philosophy and their high standards have served them well in flipping. "It creates a good name. We've had rave reviews about all of the properties we've flipped, and tenants love our rentals" Kiersten said. "We've worked hard to earn our good reputation. In this business, your reputation is everything. You're only as good as your referrals, which are key."

Kiersten Vogt's and Todd Dallas's first primary residence, a two-unit foreclosure property

Kiersten Vogt and Todd Dallas working on their live-in fixer upper in 2020

In time, Kiersten and Todd began buying properties to rent out. Today, they own eight rental properties, and they manage them all. Some of the properties are long-term rentals, where people sign a year lease. But others are short-term rentals, which Kiersten rents using Airbnb and Furnish Finder.

"You can make a lot more money on short-term rentals, but it's a lot more work," Kiersten cautioned. "Plus you have a lot of people asking you silly questions about the property, like, 'How do you turn on the air-conditioner?'"

Kiersten fields the silly questions ("Press the button on the thermostat on the wall!") and manages the properties, while Todd does all the maintenance tasks for them.

"I don't tell Todd about most of the silly questions," she said. "He doesn't have much patience for that." To try to cut down on the number of queries, Kiersten created a simple manual for her renters and leaves it strategically on the coffee table in the living room. She also emails renters a digital copy of the manual the night before their stay.

Even though the couple's short-term rentals are in Pennsburg and Pottstown, Pennsylvania, not exactly a vacation destination, they are rented out 80 to 90 percent of the time. Many of the renters are visiting nurses and other professionals who are looking for a clean, comfortable, convenient place to stay.

In addition to using the helpful tools like Airbnb, Kiersten uses a program called PriceLabs. "It's dynamic pricing, which automatically adjusts the rental rate depending upon trends," Kiersten said. "It integrates directly with Airbnb. I set it and forget it."

In 2023, Kiersten hit the books again to study for and pass her New Jersey real estate license. "The test in New Jersey is more difficult than the Pennsylvania one," she said. She wanted to get her license for New Jersey because her mom had moved to Avalon, New Jersey.

For the future, Kiersten and her husband would like to acquire more properties. "We'd like to become work-optional," she said. "But I love real estate so much I can't imagine not doing it! I'm so grateful to my parents, who showed me this way of life."

Secrets to Our Success

Overcome your fears. "Many would-be investors have analysis paralysis," Kiersten said. "To get started in real estate, you have to take a leap of faith. Just do it! Buy that first property."

Rent out what you have. "One way to get into real estate is to use

A flip project Kiersten Vogt and Todd Dallas completed in 2019

Kiersten Vogt and Todd Dallas on a cross-country road trip in 2018

your primary residence," Kiersten suggested. "My husband and I bought a house that was in foreclosure. It had three bedrooms, one bath, and an apartment above the garage. We fixed up the apartment first so we could rent it out. Then we added a fourth bedroom and second bath to make the house itself more marketable."

Get a HELOC. Ready to buy a second property? "We got a home-equity line of credit (HELOC), so we were able to take out all our renovation money, pay ourselves back for buying the property, and buy another duplex to rent," Kiersten said. "Getting a HELCO when you are the owner-occupant is so much more beneficial than getting a mortgage on a second property. You can borrow more money against the property, and banks also often give you a better interest rate."

For more information

- 215-906-7047
- Kiersten.Vogt@gmail.com
- 86 Wren Road, Gilbertsville, PA 19525
- Services offered: Residential real estate agent for buyers, sellers, and investors. Todd does residential remodeling.

Golden Lion Tamarin

We Help Families Live Better

In 2002, Maria Dattilo graduated from Immaculata University with a major in psychology and a minor in education. She obtained a master's degree in 2006 and pursued a career in counseling. Her goal was to help people by running her own psychology practice out of her home while raising her family. She had done an internship in brain injury rehabilitation, and she began work in that field after graduation. She was comfortable there, and successful.

"In 2009, I was 28 when I bought my house," said Maria. She was super excited because it felt like a big leap for a single woman. She started doing renovation projects, including ripping out old flooring and installing tile. She thought, *This is great! This is fun! I love it!* She discovered that she loved using tools and learning how to fix things. She began watching HGTV and thinking about flipping houses.

But because Maria was so comfortable in her 9-to-5 job, it took her six years to find the courage to leave and seek out a career in real estate. She told herself *If it doesn't work, it doesn't work. There's always something else.*

At first, she didn't know where to begin. She knew she wanted a broad base of knowledge before attempting to flip a house. Then she realized she could take night classes in real estate while still working full-time.

Next, Maria started researching real estate companies. First, she found a list of the top 100 companies to work for. Keller Williams was number one on the list. There were two locations nearby, so she met with the firm's recruiter. After participating in a coaching program and taking several training courses for about a year, she learned she wasn't able to do real estate only part-time. Finally, she realized, I gotta take a chance. I gotta jump in—with both feet.

So in 2014, Maria took a leap of faith, left her 9-to-5 job, and focused on real estate full-time: marketing, getting clients, and paying the bills.

Maria's father, who owned his own business, initially expressed concern over Maria entering real estate, but he saw how passionate she was about it, he said, "If you can just keep your head above water until you make it, you'll be fine. In time, you'll get there."

Marlo Jackson, Construction Supervisor, Noble Trim Contracting; Maria Dattilo, Co-Owner, Golden Lion Tamarin; Frank Dattilo, General Contractor, Noble Trim Contracting and Co-Oowner, Golden Lion Tamarin

Golden Lion Tamarin's current project in Phoenixville, Pennsylvania

Her brother, Frank Dattilo, was supportive from the very beginning, though. "When Maria first said she was going to get into real estate and flipping houses, I told her I would be her first partner."

Maria threw herself into her new venture, loving it all. In 2017, she and Frank joined forces to start their company, Golden Lion Tamarin. Then they bought and flipped their first property together—the first of many. Maria's husband also helped with the physical labor.

"Frank and I share the same goals, and we think similarly," Maria said.

Less than a year after starting Golden Lion Tamarin, Frank asked Maria's husband, Marlo, to leave his job to work with him. Frank said, "Marlo is reliable, a quick learner, and keeps it light at work. He's easy to work with and his "put pride into everything you do" attitude comes through in the finishing work. I couldn't do it without him. He's my right-hand man."

As much as Maria enjoyed her new real estate job, renovating a home was always in the back of her mind. One of her clients wanted to sell her mother's house. She warned Maria that the house needed a lot of work. She thought, *This could be the house I've been looking for.*

When Maria and Frank saw the house, it was a disaster. But in their minds, it was the brass ring. It had a ton of potential. Friends and family invested money to help them buy the lots, including their mom and Maria's father-in-law.

"I kept asking myself how we would raise the money," Maria said. "But friends and family were actually eager to invest. It felt like the money just appeared. It was incredible. I wasn't nervous, not even afraid really. I asked my friends, 'What do I have to be afraid of? This is a calculated risk. Homes have value.'

They bought the house, with the goal of fixing it up and flipping it. They hired an architect and home inspector and learned that the house needed even more work than they thought. Rather than renovate it, they simply relisted it, sold it, and made a profit.

With that money, the siblings bought a tiny three-bedroom Cape Cod. It was a perfect starter project. They fixed it up and sold it. Then, with that money, they bought a large 1900s Victorian, which needed several costly renovations. Eventually, they sold it and made a small profit.

With the profits from the sale of those first three houses, the siblings bought their first five-unit rental property. A few months later, they bought another three units. Over the next few years, they renovated and sold the five-unit, and their current project is a four-unit property in Phoenixville they are renovating to be short-term rentals.

Meanwhile, a contractor they were working with recommended finding a lot and building new houses on it. Frank and Maria found not one but two lots side-by-side in Phoenixville, Pennsylvania.

"I believed deeply that this was going to work," Maria added. "I told myself, *This is what I'm going to do,* and then I just did it. I think that's what following your dreams should be like."

"Back then I was a little nervous," Frank said. "We had a lot on the line. We were both on the loan, so if anything didn't go right, we were responsible. It was a big thing to take on, but I always tell Maria, 'Go big!' Fortune favors

Interior work by Golden Lion Tamarin in Phoenixville, Pennsylvania

The team's work on a four-unit building in Phoenixville, Pennsylvania

the bold. I figured we'll take a shot."

So they did.

Each step looked like a tall mountain to scale, but as the siblings moved along, the mountains looked smaller, probably because they were working through more and more challenges. Soon, they didn't feel like challenges anymore, just the next steps in the journey.

"When you tell yourself it's what you're going to do and you stick to it, you're committed to that idea," Maria said. "You're dedicated to it. You seek out what you need, and the answers just come. You look for the people, and they present themselves. You ask for the money, and you get it. You put it out to the universe, and then you just find a way to make it happen. Each step just presents itself."

"You can't give in to the fear of taking the risk," Maria continued. "In fact, maybe give in to the fear of regret. You don't want to regret not taking the risk later. When the fear of regret is greater than the fear of the risk, that's when you know you have to take a chance. You're ready."

After Maria and Frank built the twin houses, they found another lot, engineered it, and were approved to build four houses in the next year.

As Maria and Frank were working on getting the approvals to build those houses, Frank and his wife were at a family gathering around Thanksgiving, Frank came in from the other room and his wife said, "Oh, you're going to buy this house and flip it."

While Maria was pregnant with her first baby, she worked on a house, tiling a shower, until the day before she went into labor, thinking, *I have stuff to do. I have a house to flip!* Her mom and husband tried to convince her to "take it easy and rest," but she wanted to work. Maria's husband and Frank did a lot of the work on that property, after which Frank started his own contracting business.

They want to continue to renovate and flip houses as well as find land and build homes. They would like to take on even bigger projects, such as renovating a warehouse or church into apartments, and they would also like to do custom features to a client's liking.

"I can't imagine what the future will hold, but I see us reaching the point where my brother and I earn a full salary from our business and enough passive income to retire at 50 if we choose to!" Maria said. "We're going to keep moving forward!"

"For the future, I want to continue to 'Go big!' Frank said. "Both of us would like to gain enough rental and passive income to sustain a substantial income, and these rentals over time continue to generate wealth that we can pass on to the next generation."

Secrets to Our Success

Trust your instincts. "Looking back, it feels like this was all meant to happen in my life—in this way and at this time," Maria said. "For fourteen years, I helped people in the health-care field, but my interest in real estate and flipping houses was always there in the back of my mind. I knew I would regret it if I didn't try.

"At one point, I was dreading regret more than I was worried about taking on a new venture. That's when you know you have to take a risk. That's when it's time to jump."

Consider taking classes. Maria's real estate classes helped the pair learn, and Frank took a mastermind class with other real estate professionals and learned from networking with them. "With each project, our skills grow," Frank said. "It's always a balance of time and money. Doing things yourself might take longer, while hiring someone costs more."

For More Information

- Facebook: @NobleTrimContracting

- 215-264-2473 and 484-614-8074

- nobletrimcontracting@gmail.com, maria@dattilorealtygroup.com

- Services offered: Contracting and Real Estate

Edwing Joseph, Owner of Edwing Joseph & Sons, and his family

Edwing Joseph & Sons

Changing Lives One Suit at a Time

Edwing Joseph grew up in Port of Prince, Haiti, in the 1960s, watching his father, Edgar Joseph, create custom clothing for his clients. Growing up, Edgar had lived for several years with a tailor, and that's where he learned his craft.

"I loved seeing my dad's customers' excitement to try on their new, custom-designed clothing," Edwing said. "Their happiness made a tremendous impression on me."

But Edwing's childhood wasn't all rosy. When he was only nine years old, his family was robbed at gunpoint in their car.

"I remember that day like it was yesterday," Edwing remembered. "I was with my father, mother, aunt, brother, and sister in our car. After that, I couldn't focus at school or sleep at night. I didn't want to be in Haiti anymore."

The family traveled regularly to the United States, and during their 2000 visit, Edwing's parents told him that he wouldn't be returning to Haiti. Instead, he was going to stay in the United States and live with his aunt and uncle in Hackensack, New Jersey.

"I couldn't believe it!" Edwing said. "It felt like the best thing that ever happened to me."

Then his parents told him that they and his sister were going back to Haiti.

"Then it felt like the *worst* thing that had ever happened to me," he said.

Fortunately, Edwing's sister moved to New Jersey soon after, followed by their mother. Their father remained in Haiti, working ten times harder than he had before to support his family in the United States. In fact, he still lives in Haiti.

Edwing attended late elementary and then middle school in New Jersey. When he was in high school, he wore a suit every day. He even wore a suit to his first job interview to pump gas at a gas station. His new boss joked, "Please don't wear that tomorrow."

Growing up, Edwing used to tell people, "I'm going to own a custom suit

Edwing Joseph and his sons

shop one day." To this day, people message him to say, "I remember you used to say you were going to open your own shop, and I'm so proud you did."

After Edwing graduated from high school, he worked in jobs as varied as banking, law enforcement, and sales. But he still dreamed of owning his own shop. Although he had learned a lot by watching his father in Haiti, he had never made full suits. To gain those skills, he started work as an apprentice to other tailors, learning the ropes.

In 2014, Edwing's dream finally came true. He opened his first shop in 2014 in Vernon, New Jersey. He quickly learned that the greatest opportunity was in making suits for special events, such as proms and weddings.

"It has always made me so happy to see a man wearing a sharp suit," Edwing said. "It's much like when a car aficionado sees an expensive vehicle. I'll get butterflies in my stomach and think, 'Wow, that's nice!'"

As Edwing's shop grew, so did his family. He and his wife welcomed their first son shortly after his shop opened. Their second arrived a few years later, and their third son was born in 2022.

"I was very motivated, eager to grow my business and to be there for my wife and our sons," Edwing said.

Over the years, business was a struggle at times. Early on, Edwing began traveling to find more opportunities. He found a full-time job in Easton as an asset manager. He moved his family from New Jersey to the Lehigh Valley. Just as they were settling in to their new home, the company went under.

"I needed to start all over again," Edwing remembered. Edwing had been continuing to run his Vernon shop long-distance, and now undaunted, he began promoting his custom-tailored suits in the Lehigh Valley, too. He created a huge list of people who needed suits, such as lawyers and real estate agents, printed brochures, and literally started knocking on doors.

When no doors opened, Edwing talked with two of his friends who owned Lehigh Printing. They offered him a room to work out of in their building, in exchange for him helping them with T-shirts and doing cross-promotion. That was the ticket: Clients started coming in!

Next, Edwing was offered a larger space in the business of a church friend right on Main Street in Bethlehem. A few years later, he moved to a space in Venture X in Bethlehem.

"I was one of the first businesses at Venture X," Edwing said. "I love the ambiance there. When clients came in and saw how luxurious it is, they were very impressed."

Edwing's business quickly outgrew that space, and he moved to his current location at the intersection of East Broad and Linden Streets in Bethlehem. His company employs several salespeople, and they are often so busy they contract work out to other tailors. Today, many of the people who run the Lehigh Valley come to Edwing Joseph & Sons to have their suits made.

Speaking of the company name, even though Edwing's sons were very young, he named his company Edwing Joseph & Sons because someone once criticized him, "Hey you can't have your kids here while you're working."

"No one can ever tell me my sons can't be here," Edwing said. "They are part of my company, literally in its name."

His boys come by the shop often, watching their dad sew and sometimes even helping. Edwing is proud to give his sons the same opportunities to learn as his father gave him.

Edwing Joseph & Sons specializes in custom suits.

"Our mission at Edwing Joseph & Sons is to ensure every one of our clients walks out of our office with a suit that will transform their look. We have created custom suits for decades for Wall Street executives, NFL football players, and other people in highly distinguished positions." —Edwing Joseph

He wants his boys to see how his suits transform their looks and their lives.

"Our mission at Edwing Joseph & Sons is to ensure every one of our clients walks out of our office with a suit that will transform their look," Edwing said. "We believe our suits are a tool that will serve as a factor in their success because first impressions do last. We hope to curate an experience that will last with our customers for a long time."

Secrets to Our Success

Good tailoring is always valued. Edwing Joseph & Sons has created custom suits for decades for Wall Street executives, NFL football players, and other people in highly distinguished positions. In addition to creating brand-new suits, Edwing Joseph & Sons also tailors other makers' suits and women's clothing, too.

"As time passes, our bodies change, perhaps due to a new diet or workout regimen," Edwing explained. "It's a terrible feeling to put on your favorite piece of clothing and find out that it no longer fits. That's never a problem for our clients because we have the expertise to make a jacket or pair of pants fit like it used to, or even better. Our tailors are masters at their craft, no matter your body type or where you purchased your clothes. We'll be happy to customize your clothing to your unique size and shape."

Never underestimate the power of a good fit. Even though our culture's dress code has changed, especially after the COVID-19 pandemic, people still need formal wear. Many of life's most important occasions still warrant wearing a suit, such as weddings.

"You want to look your best on the days you'll remember most," Edwing said. "Even in today's constantly evolving world, one thing that never changes is the value of a timeless suit. A well-fitting suit is a sign of a person with good taste and distinction. With so many options only a click away, ill-fitting suits

"Never forget that you only have one opportunity to make the first impression." —Edwing Joseph

made of sub-par materials might seem like viable solutions. Yet once they're worn, their limitations are clear."

Edwing stresses that a custom-tailored suit is a wise investment in a man's future.

"You can count on our suits to help you climb to the next level you're looking to reach or provide you with the confidence to command the next room you step into. Our suits are made for you."

Give back. It takes about forty hours to custom-make a suit, and Edwing Joseph & Sons makes more than 100 suits a year. While most of their customers are people with means, they also have a tremendous heart to give to people less fortunate. Over the years, they have donated more than 200 suits to numerous foundations. Edwing is also part of an annual, weeklong program at Moravian University where local Black and Latino high school seniors attend classes about entrepreneurship and college readiness. At the end of the week, they are each gifted a new suit from the university.

"I love seeing the looks on their faces when they try on their suits," Edwing said. "There's no better feeling than putting on a suit for the first time."

In the future, Edwing hopes to continue growing his business and also encouraging and supporting other people to follow their dreams.

"I know how hard it was for me to build my business and this life," he said. "I could have gone many different routes, but because I had so many good people in my life and because God led me on the right path, I chose the right path. I've learned that I love to help other people. I want to be like a lighthouse, helping others to see the right path for them."

For More Information

- www.EdwingJSons.com

EDWING JOSEPH & SONS
CHANGING LIVES ONE SUIT AT A TIME

- 201-228-0616

- clients@edwingjsons.com

- Book an appointment: www.EdwingJSons.com or call/text 201-228-0616

- 302 East Broad Street, 1st Floor, Bethlehem, PA 18018 (The entrance is on Linden Street.)

- Services offered: Custom and tailored clothing

Robbins Rehabilitation West

Not many people can say they knew what they wanted to do with their life in high school. But when Travis Robbins was injured playing high school basketball—then helped by physical therapy, he thought, *Maybe I could do this for my life.*

After high school graduation, Travis attended Ithaca College, where he met his college sweetheart, Amanda. While Travis took the five-year master's program in physical therapy, Amanda majored in communications and broadcasting—then studied speech pathology and got a master's in education. Even though Travis was two years ahead of Amanda in school, one semester they had two classes together.

After graduation, the couple was living in Boston. They had been house-hunting, and were dismayed by the real estate prices in the city. One weekend, they drove to visit Travis' brother in New Jersey. When the topic of conversation turned to real estate, Travis' brother pulled out a newspaper flyer advertising cheap houses in the Poconos.

"We had never even heard of the Poconos, but it was on our way home, so we went into a real estate office. We bought a house that day," Amanda remembered.

Travis and Amanda lived in the Poconos for a few years. Their daughter was born in 2005.

One day, Travis opened up the newspaper and saw a job posting for a physical therapist in Allentown in a large, corporate physical therapy practice. The work was rewarding, but the commute was not. Travis worked from 7 am to 7 pm two days a week, so he left home before their baby was up and didn't get back until after she had gone to sleep at night.

"I didn't want to do that anymore," Travis said. So they began looking for a place near Allentown to live. After they moved, Travis opened his own

At right: Travis and Amanda Robbins, Owners of Robbins Rehabilitation West

In physical therapy as a whole, the success rate of people who complete their entire plan of care is 11 percent. The success rate at Robbins Rehabilitation West? 80 to 92 percent.

practice, renting space from a chiropractor who wanted to have a physical therapist in his office.

"So then I started working 7 am to 7 pm every day," Travis laughed. "I opened up my own place about a year after that, Robbins Rehabilitation."

Two years later, Travis' identical twin brother, who is also a physical therapist, joined him in the practice. The brothers worked together for a while. Five years ago, they divided the practice into Robbins West, covering the Lehigh Valley and Bangor, run by Travis, and Robbins East, covering Easton and New Jersey and run by his brother.

The couple's older son was born in 2006, then a daughter in 2009, and another son in 2011. Before the children were born, Amanda was a teacher. She stayed home with them when they were young. But by the time their youngest was in first grade, Amanda was ready to go back to work.

"I didn't want to go back to teaching because I needed more flexibility than that can offer," Amanda said. So she joined the business. "I do all of the finances, metrics, human resources—the administrative side," she said. "My role is flexible, which is helpful with four young children who are busy with school and activities. On the other hand, Travis runs the clinical side."

Robbins Rehab West has grown quickly from one clinic location to four— Upper Macungie; Allentown across from Lehigh Valley Health Network; Bethlehem on Schoenersville Road; and Bangor.

They have a second company called Phoenix Practice Management, which manages the physical therapists in two doctors' offices. Those clinics are each run by boots-on-the-ground clinical directors who have been physical therapists with the company for as long as 13 years.

Up until recently, Travis was focused mainly on onboarding, training, and educating staff at Robbins. He also owns several other companies. One, Physical Therapy Billing, is a billing and collection company with small-

The Robbins family: Cade, Macy, Delaney, Harrison, Travis, and Amanda

private practice clients all over the United States. Another, Next Level PT Consulting Company, is a coaching practice for physical therapists in private practice.

Running not one but four family businesses can be daunting, even for a couple as efficient and effective as Amanda and Travis. But they have a well-trained staff to help.

At times, their kids have also pitched in. "Before our oldest daughter went away to the Fashion Institute of Technology in New York City, she helped me a lot with the metrics," Amanda said. "It's critically important as a small business to watch our numbers closely to make sure we are seeing enough patients to cover our payroll and expenses."

"Travis is always looking to create the best environment for our employees. Happy employees equals happy patients."

—Amanda Robbins

Robbins Rehabilitation West staff, family, and friends delivering turkeys to various shelters, food pantries, Salvation Armies, and YMCAs across the Lehigh Valley

The other kids help with tasks like folding up a T-shirt order. "We give a T-shirt to each patient after they complete their plan of care," Travis explained.

Speaking of that patient plan of care, it's surprising to learn that in physical therapy as a whole, the success rate of people who complete their entire plan of care is 11 percent. The success rate at Robbins Rehab West? 80 to 92 percent.

Secrets to Our Success

Enter with an exit plan. "You need to have an exit plan," Travis said. "I remember when I first started, someone mentioned developing an exit plan, and I thought, *I'm going to do this until I die.* But as you get older, you realize you really do need an exit strategy."

Diversify. Much about a physical therapy practice is dictated by insurance companies. Over the years, physical therapists have seen their compensation from insurance companies go lower and lower and lower. One way to fight that trend is to avoid putting all of your eggs in one basket. That's why Travis and Amanda started their second, third, and fourth family businesses. If one of their endeavors is struggling, they can ramp up another!

Running not one but four family businesses can be daunting, even for a couple as efficient and effective as Amanda and Travis. But they have a well-trained staff to help.

Foster a great environment for your employees. "Travis is always looking to create the best environment for our employees," Amanda said. "Happy employees equals happy patients."

"Something I'm really proud of is our aide program," Travis said. "Our aids are the entry-level position. It's the hardest job that we have. But it gives young adults experience in the physical therapy field to help them to be successful in school. Over the past year, we sent seven young adults to PT school. It's so cool to see that. We've been doing that for 20 years."

And people in the Lehigh Valley struggling with injuries hope the team at Robbins Rehab West continues their excellent work for at least 20 more.

For More Information

- www.RobbinsPTWest.com

- 610-841-3555

- amanda@robbinsptwest.com

- Street addresses:
  - 1245 S. Cedar Crest Blvd., Suite 205, Allentown, PA 18103
  - 6750 Iroquois Trail 12A, Allentown, PA 18104
  - 3535 Medical Drive, Suite 300, Bethlehem, PA 18017
  - 225 Erdman Avenue (Inside the MultiCare Plus), Bangor, PA 18013

- Services offered: Physical and rehabilitative therapy

Troy Good and sons Jacob and Brandon

Troy Good Roofing and Good Family Investors LLC

Our Business Grew from Roofing to Real Estate

Troy Good grew up in Boyertown, the youngest of four. Right out of high school, he started working construction jobs. He worked for a contractor for a few years, but when the contractor moved to western Pennsylvania, Troy felt led to start his own business, even though he was only twenty-one-years old and lacked the necessary experience in business and the industry.

Troy knew he lacked experience, so he sometimes solicited the help of older, more experienced contractors to help him bid on certain jobs that he did not have as much experience with. When he got those jobs, he would hire the contractors as subs to help him. This provided the homeowner with a professional job and at the same time gave Troy added experience and was promoting and building his business.

Even with help and support, it was a stressful time for the fledgling business.

"When I started my company, people seemed to be so excited for me, and I thought I had three to four weeks of work lined up," Troy remembered. "That turned out to be three to four *days*, and I finished it in just two. It was hard lining up work. When I would go to people's homes to create an estimate for a project, I could see the fear in their eyes. They knew I was young, and they guessed correctly that I was inexperienced. It can be scary to have any contractor come into your house and start ripping things apart—let alone a young, baby-faced contractor."

In time, Troy's confidence grew, and his clients' confidence in him grew as well. When things were slow, Troy cold-called potential clients, and he reached out to other contractors to see if they could use them. They often could. Good-paying work led to more good-paying work.

After a few years, Troy's business was busy enough to necessitate that he hire a helper. But then in 2008, the economy crashed.

"I remember I was sitting in my tree stand hunting, and I though to myself *I have two days of work left*," Troy said. "I texted people all over the place—as far away as Louisiana. Within 24 hours, I was on my way to North Carolina for the closest work I could find."

That was when Troy realized he needed a wider, larger pipeline of incoming work. Having work come in from multiple sources and areas makes a business more stable. For example, if the company was getting most of its work from one little town and then for some reason the town had an economic downturn, they would be in trouble. So Troy knew that he needed to expand his business's reach. In that time, he also realized that the more time he spent off the job, the more his business grew. This concept was hard to learn because he was very much a do-it-yourselfer. So he slowly replaced himself on the jobsite and worked himself off the job.

Then he was invited to a network meeting that was enlightening.

"Out of the fifteen businesspeople in the room, I was the only contractor," he said. "The others were thrilled to have a contractor there. I left that breakfast meeting with six viable job leads. I realized networking worked!"

After that, Troy began to do more networking.

"My goal was to try build a scalable business," he explained. "A lot of contractors are good at a trade, and they fall into being businesspeople. But they're not actually businesspeople, they're craftspeople. Often, people become frustrated with contractors because they don't communicate well or run their business well. That's because they lack business training. They only know how to work in their jobs. That's all-consuming to them. And worst of all, they can't grow because they have no idea how to scale their business because they *are* their business."

Truth be told, Troy's own first attempt at scaling didn't go as hoped. He hired six workmen to be able to take on more work, but after a year or two, he was making only a little more money—for a lot more effort.

"Years ago, a mentor told me, 'You can hammer 100 nails a day, but if you hire someone, he's only going to hammer in 80. Another guy might only hammer in 70. The more people you're managing, the less efficient it becomes.'"

Mulling over that piece of advice, around that time, Troy brought the oldest

Good Family Investors, LLC at a settlement

of his five children (three boys, two girls), his son Brandon on as part-owner of Good Contracting. This allowed Troy to pivot. He eased most of his workers out. He had realized that roofing was an area that the company could most easily scale their business with because his son could oversee the jobs without having to actually do all the work, often more than one job at a time. So this allowed the company to accomplish more work in less time with fewer full-time employees. So he thought, *If I can find a subcrew to help me do roofs, I could do plenty of them.* Troy trained Brandon to communicate with a customer and get the crew started on the roof, then move on to another job, then another, then another. That was the key to scaling the business.

All this time Troy was busy building his contracting business, he had also ventured into another income stream: real estate investing. By the late 1990s, he had bought about twenty-five units in Berks County. As a contractor, he was able to do all the improvements and maintenance himself.

But it came at a high price: His wife hated it. Can you blame her? She was at home raising their five young kids, and the added pressure of tenants, building maintenance, and additional financial responsibility was overwhelming.

So between 2005 and 2006, Troy sold all those properties, coincidentally at the very top of the market.

"I looked like a genius," he laughed. "But it was the right timing."

Troy stayed out of the real estate market for a while. But then a friend encouraged him to invest in properties in Reading. He joined the real estate group REIA to learn about the market, then bought a short-sale property in 2010 and another in 2012.

"These properties just happened to fall in my lap," he said.

Then in 2018, Troy went to a real estate meetup. The large room was filled with investors and flippers—but few contractors.

"I was suddenly very popular," Troy said.

That night, everyone in the group wanted to talk to Troy as soon as they found out he was a contractor. He started attending some meetings and soon decided that it was time for him to dip his feet back into real estate investing, but this time it would be different. This time he would not try to do everything himself but would delegate as much as possible so that he could do more. It was a lesson he had already learned in his construction business.

So Troy began buying more and more properties, and he's purchased sixty properties since then. He flips some and rents out others. At that time, Troy's son Jacob was starting to get interested in real estate and would watch real estate-related webinars and reels. One time in particular, he invited Brandon over to watch a webinar about real estate. Brandon and his wife already owned a three-unit in Pottstown. Afterward, they decided they wanted to buy real estate together. Shortly after that, they approached Troy about working with them to build a real estate portfolio. The three started meeting every Monday morning at 6 am to start discussing all the details. Out of that came Good Family Investors LLC.

Working on a reno project

"A week later we had our first property under contract, and in the first year we bought twelve properties."

Troy has helped other investors start four or five real estate meetup groups in northeast Pennsylvania and helps run one in Schuylkill county, where some of Good Family Investors investments are located. He also travels around to speak on the topic of contractors: How to find, vet, and work with your contractor to get your flip or renovation to the finish line. As the family's real estate business has gotten bigger, they have narrowed the focus of their contracting. Now they work primarily on roofing, windows, and decks.

"Working with my sons is a joy," Troy said. "I've always designed my life and career around doing what I enjoy and what I felt called to do. So I didn't *push* my kids to work with me. But I always tell them what a privilege it is to work with them and how happy it makes me."

Even though Troy's youngest son doesn't work in the family business right now, he still played an important part. He decided to move to Tennessee and had a job lined up. Troy's advice?

"I think you'll hate the job, but I think you should go. It's a great opportunity to learn. I'll take you down and help you move."

Two weeks before the drive, Troy though he'd see if he could meet some real estate people in Tennessee, so he joined a bunch of Facebook groups. He posted, "I'm an investor from Pennsylvania coming down to potentially buy some properties." People reached out asking if he could speak about contracting. "Wholesalers and Realtors reached out to me," Troy said. "I came up with the idea to plan a real estate meetup in Chattanooga where I would speak on how to find, vet, and work with contractors to get their flips and rehabs to the finish line!" It was a huge success with more than forty agents and investors in attendance. Troy made great connections, which put his idea of building a real estate portfolio in Tennessee on the fast track!

Before heading back to Pennsylvania, Troy was asked to speak at another meetup in Nashville by someone who saw the advertisement for the Chattanooga meeting. The importance of the contractor piece of real estate investing is drastically overlooked by new real estate investors. Seasoned investors know the importance of it and are excited to learn how they can better deal with contractors. Two days later, on Troy's way back to Pennsylvania, he stopped by Nashville to speak to another group. He regularly travels to speak at groups to help others and at the same time build his network.

In addition to the three sons, Troy's two daughters are also involved in the family business. Brittany's husband, Seth, is currently partnering with Troy on a flip project that is closer to where they live. This allows Troy to expand his business in another area as well as help his daughter and son-in-law earn some extra money. His daughter Grace, who is still in college, helps Troy and his bookkeeper manage the apartments, and she might be adding more to her plate in the future.

"It was a great way to connect with many investors at once," Troy said.

In the future, Troy hopes to continue to expand the family business, while easing himself out, making room for his sons to succeed and thrive.

Secrets to Our Success

Network. "I've become a serial networker," Troy said. "That's what I do best. Other people tell me they have a hard time finding properties to buy. But because of my network, I hear about so many of them, I can't keep up with them! A man literally came up to me on the street, having recognized me from Facebook, and I ended up buying a property from him. I bought another property from the cousin of a lady I met at Carpet Mart."

Be a people person. "Growing up, I was quiet and shy," Troy said. "But I've always loved people, and I've become much more of an extrovert over the years. Growing up, my mentor was a man who came from humble beginnings to become very successful. The secret to his success? He was a master at working with people. Eighty percent of the time, people hire people that they like. Do what you can to increase your emotional intelligence."

Take care of people. The best way to become a people person is to take care of people. "In business, you have to be tough, but you can also be nice," Troy said. Once, Troy hired a tenant to help him gather firewood. On the way to the location, Troy realized the tenant hadn't eaten anything, and he had clearly lost weight from not eating. So Troy stopped by his house, took the tenant inside, packed them some lunches, and took the tenant and Troy's sons to gather firewood for the day. At the end of the day, Troy took the tenant out for dinner, paid him for the day, and dropped him off at his apartment.

For More Information

- 610-468-3848
- Instagram: troy_l_good
  goodcontractingllc
  goodfamilyinvestorsllc

- Facebook: Troy Good
  Good Contracting LLC
  Good Family Investors LLC
- Services offered: Contracting, roofing, investing

MVP Cleaning

We Clean and Organize—So You Don't Have To

Parthenia Mungin grew up in the south in the small town of Tarboro, Georgia, with her parents and three younger brothers. Because her mother was a nurse and her father owned his own construction company but his family worked in law enforcement, Parthenia thought she might like to be a pediatric nurse or lawyer.

"My three goals were to found an orphanage, open a nursing home, and have ten children," Parthenia remembered. "I still hope to have an orphanage and nursing home someday—but my three daughters keep me plenty busy."

Growing up, Parthenia always dreamed of becoming a business owner. She honed her skills cleaning, organizing, planning, and leading from an early age, taking care of her brothers.

"My parents both worked, and I was always the caretaker in our home," she said. "I was always cooking, cleaning, babysitting, and driving my brothers somewhere. My role as 'stewardess' wasn't something I thought much about. It was my responsibility, and I simply accepted it. I did it with happiness."

Parthenia and her father were especially close. "I was the apple of his eye," she said with a smile. "Daddy's girl." Her dad helped her with homework and took her shopping and even to the hair salon, while her mother focused more on her brothers. Parthenia's father is also a pastor, and he read to her for hours. While he is kind, he was also exacting, saying, "If you want to do something, give it 100 percent, or don't bother doing it at all."

Even though Parthenia grew up in a loving home, she yearned to spread her wings and gain her independence. Her first daughter was born in Georgia in 1998. Then at Southeast Georgia Community College, she rebelled completely, pushing back against her straight-laced parents. When she met the man she perceived to be a knight in shining armor, Parthenia moved with him first to Orlando, Florida, then almost 1,000 miles away to New York City.

"My dad had tried to warn me that he was a bad actor, but I wanted to be my own person," Parthenia said. "I needed to find out for myself."

At right, Back: Parthenia Mungin, Owner of MVP Cleaning.
Front: Jasmine Mungin, Joanna Lubin, and Jadah Lubin

Parthenia Mungin, Owner of MVP Cleaning

Parthenia quickly realized, "Toto, I've got a feeling we're not in Georgia anymore." She attended more college at Florida Metropolitan University. Parthenia's two younger daughters were born in New York City in 2002 and 2004. Despite those highlights, Parthenia didn't enjoy city life nearly as much as she had hoped. Plus the luster came off the knight's armor pretty quickly. He became very physically, mentally, and spiritually abusive. But because Parthenia was a stay-at-home mom at the time without an income of her own, her options for leaving were slim to none.

One day, the family wanted to go to shopping at Wal-Mart. Turns out the closest store at the time was in Pennsylvania. So they drove out to the Lehigh Valley.

"I fell in love with it right away," Parthenia said. "Compared with the noisy, dirty big city, it felt much more like the country I grew up in. Pennsylvania felt like home. Right then I knew I didn't want to raise my daughters in New York."

After living in New York City for a few months, the family moved to Allentown in December 2005. Parthenia did her best to make their relationship work until 2010, when the turmoil had become too much to bear.

In 2010, Parthenia moved with her daughters to Bath. Because she had no practical work experience, she went to a staffing agency called HTSS. They gave her a fresh start. Soon she had plenty of work opportunities and experience, working jobs as varied as trucking dispatcher, mortgage loan preparer, office manager, home health aide, even supervisor at the Laury's Station post office.

Parthenia's work experience boosted her confidence and greatly added to her skills repertoire. Although she enjoyed her work for other people, she still longed to start her own business.

And in 2017 she did.

Parthenia opened her own cleaning company, MVP Cleaning—named to emphasize that her clients are all the "most valuable people" to her.

"Only God knows how happy I've been since then," Parthenia said with a big smile.

A caretaker by nature, Parthenia knew she wanted to open a business that helped other people. Opening her own cleaning company seemed like the perfect fit because it would enable Parthenia to help others, yet still to be independent—to be her own boss, yet still to serve others.

"I was teaching myself how to clean my parents' house as soon as I was big enough to pick up a dust pan," she said.

"Today, it's an incredible privilege to go into people's home, their personal space, and to clean for them. I work hard to gain their trust. And I take the responsibility very seriously."

Another benefit to cleaning is the feeling it gives Parthenia—and her clients. "I love seeing a clean space," she said. "I like to say 'Cleanliness is next to Godliness.'"

"My faith plays an important role in all that I do," Parthenia said. "I always ask God to bless my hands and my mind. I ask Him to help me see past the chaos to make my clients' homes clean and organized. I say, "Let me see through Your eyes so I can make this the best place for the family that lives here.'"

One of Parthenia's special gifts is the ability to see what needs to be cleaned—and to clean them professionally well. Another gift is to see what needs to be organized—and to transform chaos into clean organization.

The MVP Cleaning Team: Joanna Lubin, Jadah Lubin, Jasmine Mungin, and Parthenia Mungin

Joanna Lubin, Parthenia Mungin, and Jasmine Mungin, wearing her infamous cat ears

"A person's surroundings directly reflects what's going on in the inside," Parthenia said. "And likewise, a person's surroundings also impact what's going on in the inside. Being in a chaotic space makes you feel chaos inside. And on the flip side, being in a messy space indicates a messy internal life." Helping her clients' homes get—and stay—clean and organized benefits them in so many ways—with improved mental and physical health, relationships, and even finances.

"When you clean and take care of your things properly, you don't need to replace them as often," Parthenia said.

One thing that makes MVP Cleaning unique is their focus on cleaning their clients' homes the way *they* want them to be cleaned. Unlike some cleaners, who have set cleaning products, procedures, and schedules that cannot be deviated from, Parthenia adapts her products, procedures, and schedules to suit her clients. It's not a cookie-cutter approach.

"Some cleaners say 'I clean your home the way I would clean my own,' but what's more important is 'I clean your home the way you would want to clean your home if you could.' It's akin to the difference between the golden rule (treat other people the way you would like to be treated) with the platinum rule (treat other people the way *they* want to be treated).

Everyone has their particular way of cleaning. As a cleaner, I need to understand and respect that. I always respect people and their space. I'm careful to give them what they ask for.

"I want my clients to come back to a home that feels cleaned the way they would have cleaned it. I hope they walk in and think, "Wow, it's clean!" I don't want them to walk in the door and think, "Parthenia cleaned."

A tremendous help with that is Parthenia's photographic memory. When she picks up or moves items to clean them, she's able to replace them exactly where the customer had them—to the millimeter! That way, the customer doesn't spend her first fifteen minutes at home adjusting all of her things and decorations the way she "likes them."

Other tremendous helps to MVP Cleaning have been her three daughters, Jadah, Joanna, and Jasmine, who have pitched in to help very often over the years. They also meet most of MVP Cleaning's clients, further helping to establish that like-family relationship.

"My daughters are very hard workers," Parthenia said. "And they also care deeply about our customers."

In the future, Parthenia hopes to open a cleaning academy to teach people how to clean properly. She also wants to expand her business so she can offer more career opportunities to others, especially mothers with young children who sometimes struggle to find good-paying jobs. Most of all, Parthenia hopes to write a book filled with her top cleaning tips and observations as cleaner. She wants to literally write the book on cleaning!

Secrets to Our Success

Face your fears by focusing on the benefits. Two years after I started working at the post office, I knew for sure I wanted to be my own boss. I didn't want to work a 9-5-job for someone else for the rest of my life.

Yet I was scared to walk away from the steady paycheck and benefits. I focused my eyes on the benefits to being my own boss—my independence, greater opportunity for advancement, and greater flexibility to spend time with my family. That focus on the benefits kept me from fretting about the fears.

Be a life-long learner. No matter where she lived, Parthenia has always been taking classes. After moving to the Lehigh Valley, she attended Lehigh County Community College. Today, she attends Devry University, and she plans to receive her bachelor's degree in business administration with a concentration in accounting in 2024.

Despite Parthenia's busy work schedule and family life, she's received dean's list status three tiimes.

Build strong relationships. Most people might not think they have a relationship with their housecleaner. Most might not even *see* their housecleaner because she cleans their home while they are at work.

That's not Parthenia's style. "I like to build relationships with my clients," she said. I talk with them, and more importantly I listen to them to learn what they need and want. Most of my clients have been with me for three, four, or even more years. I have a very low turnover rate."

For More Information

- 610-938-1139

- pml3379@gmail.com

- PO Box 342 Orefield, PA 18069

- Services offered: Residential and commercial cleaning, move out/move in cleaning, deep cleaning, and organizing

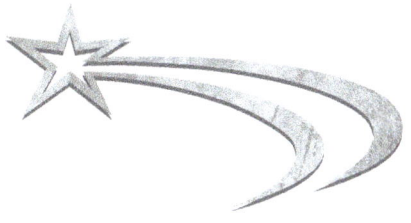

Twisted Olive

Our Casual-Style Bistro Offers a World Twist

Steve Kershner's enthusiasm for cooking began as a child, when he enjoyed time in the kitchen with his father, who was also a chef at his parents' restaurant in Emmaus.

"Cooking is in Steve's blood," said Steve's wife, Sherri. "He has worked in the restaurant business his entire life."

Steve's first job outside of the family business was at the Hotel Bethlehem. He continued to develop his unique cuisine at the hotel and then in positions at Cascade Lodge, Spring Valley Inn, Belmont Inn, and the Apollo Grill. Steve had the honor of participating in a class at La Varenne at the Green Briar Hotel with Anne Willan and Julia Child, where he was able to further hone his skills.

Sherri Beam-Kershner grew up in Danielsville, not too far from Steve in Emmaus. The pair met in a kitchen in the early 2000s.

"We were at an open house charity fundraiser, and a friend took me back to meet the kitchen staff," Sherri remembered.

Sherri is a cyber security expert, and she often travels internationally. In fact, she was traveling when Steve called to ask her out. When she said she was in Italy, Steve replied, "I haven't heard that excuse before."

Despite Sherri's jet-setting career and Steve's busy restaurant schedule, the pair still found time to date and then marry. From the beginning, they have always enjoyed shopping and cooking together.

"We love to experiment," Sherri said. "My favorite times are when we shop together to select ingredients, then cook together to make something that's fantastic. Being creative in the kitchen is one of my favorite things to do."

Sometimes the couple takes the time to write down their creations—to hold onto and later enhance. Other times, the dishes are just a pleasant memory.

Steve is well known for his talents in saving struggling restaurants and for his unparallel cooking. Sherri suggested one day, "Why are you working so hard for everyone else? If you're going to work so hard, why not work for yourself?"

At left: Sherri Beam-Kershner, Co-Owner of Twisted Olive

Steve Kershner, Co-Owner of Twisted Olive

"His food is fantastic and combined with his restaurant industry knowledge and my business and travel experience with my customer perspective, we could bring both worlds together and create a terrific restaurant," Sherri said.

The Twisted Olive opened its doors in 2013, a dream come true for both Steve and Sherri. The name was inspired by their favorite restaurant, the Black Olive, in Baltimore, Maryland. The idea was to convey a fresh, fun, approachable image to their guests.

Steve selected the restaurant's menu to further affirm that image. He didn't want to be tied to any one type of cuisine nor to limit his guests' choices. Therefore, he decided that offering an array of styles from all over the world would suit everyone best.

"On any given night, you might find Italian, Spanish, Moroccan, or Thai dishes," Steve said. "Our ideas stay fresh, so that guests will continue to come back for more."

The Twisted Olive is also home to some of the best house infusions around. In fact, it was one of the earliest restaurants to offer them. The inspiration for the infusions came from Sherri's many overseas travels.

"Because I travel so often, I know what it feels like to go to a new restaurant," Sherri said. "I'm frequently a customer. I want to have all of our guests have the same high level of experience I have in the best restaurants I get to try when I travel."

The creative mind of their very talented bartenders has brought this full-service bar to an entirely new level. With consistently changing house infusion flavors, a creative mix of house cocktails, and a great atmosphere, the Twisted Olive has become quite the spot for people looking to broaden their horizons. Of course, their guests can always enjoy the classics, too!

The creativity at Twisted Olive extends beyond their food. Sherri and Steve support local artists by featuring them for eight weeks shows.

"One hundred percent of the proceeds from those sales goes to the artists," Sherri explained.

A culinary creation from Twisted Olive

In recognition of Steve Kershner's friendly demeanor and enticing meals, he was voted Lehigh Valley's Favorite Chef by readers of Lehigh Valley Style magazine three times —in 2009, 2011, and 2014.

In addition to supporting artists, Steve and Sherri have a heart to help local nonprofit organizations as well.

"In the future, as our business continues to grow, I hope to be able to support even more artists and charities," Sherri said. "We've done a number of things to support local charities. For example, I'm part of the Northeast Community Center. I'm on the giving circles for both Good Shepard and Charter Arts."

The restaurant's creativity has brought customers from both near and far. Over the years, Steve has been privileged to have the opportunity to prepare meals for Lech Walesa, Diana Krall, Henny Youngman, Eartha Kitt, Emeril Lagasse, and Gene Kranz—NASA Flight Director for more than sixty space missions, including Apollo 11 and 13.

In recognition of Steve's friendly demeanor and enticing meals, he was voted Lehigh Valley's Favorite Chef by readers of *Lehigh Valley Style* magazine three times—in 2009, 2011, and 2014.

The inspiration for his unique dishes comes from many sources, including his travels throughout Europe. He insists on a blend of fresh ingredients, creativity, attention to detail and the utmost quality in every meal he serves. Steve devotes time to create a unique dining experience for his guests at the Twisted Olive.

"Since the beginning we always envisioned bringing the freshest most local ingredients into the kitchen at Twisted Olive," Sherri said. "Our organic GMO-free garden is a labor of love that enriches our menu, our cocktails, and our lives. From the plotting and planning in early February to the end of harvest season in late October, we are continuously looking for ways to allow our customers to experience the freshest ingredients. From our handcrafted cocktails to our bountiful menu, the garden works its way into our daily activities. This allows us to pass on the fruits of our labor to our customers."

Twisted Olive worked especially hard to help and to serve its customers

during the Covid-19 pandemic. The restaurant added to-go family meals to its menu, which were so popular they are still on the menu. They also expanded their outdoor seating and added plenty of heaters. For a brief time, they were even allowed to serve their famous cocktails to go!

"Right now, the restaurant is known for its French Onion Dumplings," Sherri said. "Also, Steve's Braised Shortrib Ravioli with a Madeier Cream Sauce is fabulous, and his crabcakes are phenomenal."

Twisted Olive specializes in global cuisine.

As many ingredients as possible are sourced from the restaurant's own gardens. As of this writing, the fig trees were bountiful with figs, helping to bring the taste of Italy to Twisted Olive's tables. Beyond the restaurant's gardens, they also source many ingredients from local farmers. Some of those farmers have grow tunnels, which greatly expand their growing season.

"Please visit, sit back, and enjoy your time here," Steve said. "It would be our pleasure to have you dining with us."

Secrets to Our Success

Go the extra mile. Steve and Sherri work hard to build connections and relationships with their customers, garnering a wide, loyal following. For example, recently they surprised a "regular" family by making their daughter's favorite burrito while she was home visiting from college.

For More Information

- www.TwistedOliveBethlehem.com

- 610-419-1200

- u097sbeam@yahoo.com

- 51 West Broad Street, Bethlehem, PA 18018

- Services offered: Food from around the world with a twist

Silent Partner
Insurance Solutions

We Help Families Make Smart Medicare Decisions

Back in the 1990s, Maria Santacoloma was working in the taxing and travel-heavy cosmetics and fragrance industry. She was about to get married—and could no longer be "married" to her job. Her new husband, Manny Santacoloma, was supportive as she started her own company, Silent Partner Marketing, to help companies that didn't know how to market themselves. Maria and Manny began their life together in Cooper City, Florida, at the time, though they both hailed from New York.

Then, Maria was offered an opportunity in Pennsylvania that seemed too good to pass up. Even though Maria really didn't want to give up working for herself, the couple now had a son, named Matthew, and they were eager to raise him near friends and family. The job offer and timing felt serendipitous for them all.

"Little did I know, the company was not in a good situation when they hired me," Maria remembered. "It was a seventy-five-year-old company, so it seemed like a great opportunity. They gave me a VP title, a nice office, a tremendous salary, bonuses, and a car. They made many promises, but the business shut down less than two years after I started. I got my walking papers on Matthew's third birthday."

Nothing can cause you to pivot like panic, and Maria thought on her feet. "I had no network in Pennsylvania, no work connections because I had to fire my entire in-house marketing team. My eight-month severance was going to go quickly. So I asked myself, *What can I sell or market to make myself valuable and self-employed?* I came up with something that everyone needs: insurance."

Maria studied for and passed her insurance license in 2004, and she began selling health insurance. Her new business had a new mission, but a familiar name: Silent Partner Insurance Solutions.

At right: Manny, Maria, and Matthew Santacoloma of Silent Partner Insurance Solutions

Just as Maria was finding her footing, she had to pivot again.

"In 2010, the Affordable Care Act took insurance agents out of the mix," she said. "People could now go online and buy their own insurance."

Manny offered comforting words: "We've pivoted before. We're not anyplace we haven't been before. Let's figure this out."

Fortunately, this was a smaller adjustment. Maria remained in the insurance industry, just shifted her focus onto Medicare. She quickly became one of the top-selling independent agents in the entire state of Pennsylvania. She was so successful, United Healthcare kept offering her on-staff positions. *No. No. I'm never doing that again*, she thought, vowing to stay self-employed.

Maria was highly successful, selling close to 300 Medicare plans each year. So United Healthcare got creative in their offering: "They said, 'If you won't come work for us, we have another opportunity. Become an independent marketing office.'"

That was the perfect blend for Silent Partner. They could *keep* their book of business and renewals, but they could also *hire* a team of independent agents who would benefit from their support. Maria would recruit them and train them. This was ideal because she had grown too busy to take on new clients herself—except for current clients and referrals. This was the winning formula, and the company has already celebrated its tenth anniversary—with seventy-five agents on their team. They're currently United Healthcare's number two IMO agency in sales, and they are the second largest independent marketing office in the country.

Today, Maria is still the face of the company, prospecting and networking every day. Manny runs the back office. Behind the scenes, he manages scheduling, qualifying, paperwork processing, and the website and branding.

Despite their different daily tasks, one thing they both have in common is a love of helping people.

"When I visit some of the seniors in their homes, I find many of them just want a friend to talk to," Maria said. "I am still in contact with many of my very first clients. I will receive email of new grandbabies being born or sometimes sad news of their spouse passing. During those calls, we spend time together making sure they are okay. That's often when I rely on my community partners like Care Patrol (see page 38), Fox Rehab, VA assistance through the county office and Meals On Wheels to help find resources for my clients."

Maria and Manny especially like helping seniors grappling with tough insurance decisions. They encourage people to reach out three months before they turn sixty-five.

"We don't discourage anyone from reaching out before age sixty-five. We like to educate them about their Medicare options. I love to say, 'Let's do the math. It all comes down to health and wealth.'" —Maria Santacoloma

"But we don't discourage anyone from reaching out earlier," Maria said. "We like to educate them about their Medicare options. I love to say, 'Let's do the math. It all comes down to health and wealth.'"

Maria's goal is to help people to preserve as much wealth as possible for their retirement. Many agents on her team are financial planners who can help seniors plan for retirement. Agents also network with other organizations that help seniors, such as CarePatrol and Fox Rehab. They are members of Lehigh Valley Aging in Place. Maria is also a board member of Lehigh Valley Active Life and is part of the Lehigh Valley Health Network Auxiliary.

"Lehigh Valley Aging in Place is a coalition of senior focused businesses throughout the region," Maria explained. "I have been part of this group, as well as a former Board Member, and have chaired several events with them. This has made me a stronger resource for my client base, in getting them the help and services they often times did not know existed."
"We try to help age in place," Maria said. "It's important to factor Medicare into your planning because if you move to a senior community, you have to have a plan that's going to work with that community."

Speaking of communities, Maria and her team regularly visit local senior communities to meet with seniors there. "We review plans with the residents, making sure they are on the right one for them," Maria said. "We often stay all day and give free half-hour appointments."

Interestingly, it's not always necessary to go *to* the seniors anymore to educate them because they are getting better at educating themselves.

"Seniors are getting 'younger,' Maria explained. "A person turning 65 today has had access to computers for a really long time. She's likely into social media—not just for her grandkids but for herself. She's very savvy. Many seniors today do their own research."

I wear my nametag everywhere, even while running errands to Wegmans and Target,. When people see it, they ask me questions about Medicare and AARP. Many seniors want to know about AARP and United because they are strong brands they trust!

—Maria Santacoloma

Still they might reach out to Silent Partner for their expert perspective. "Researching online is like drinking from a firehouse," Maria cautions. "There's so much information out there, and it's definitely not all correct."

Maria offers plenty of information, but what she can't offer is advice or make decisions for people.

"People ask me all the time, 'What would *you* do ?'" Maria said. "I don't suggest. I present the information on the different plans, and I can help show how they work. But I don't have a crystal ball to predict what they might need in the future. I can ask questions, though, to learn more about their past and what they *have* needed. For instance I'll ask, How often do you go to the doctor? How many specialists do you see? Would you be more comfortable paying a monthly premium or a higher copay?"

Another way the Silent Partner team educates and informs people is by holding Medicare seminars all throughout the year, especially during annual enrollment season, which is October 15 through December 7, with the marketing season beginning October 1. The team holds seminars in many convenient locations in the Lehigh Valley, including YMCAs, JCCs, gyms, Meals on Wheels, and private clubs. Their territory is all of Eastern Pennsylvania up to the New York border. Silent Partner is also licensed in 15 states.

The company is hoping to continue to grow even more. It just added a fourth down line in Delaware, which means there are now four agencies under their team. They can promote agents from within, and those agents can create their own agency. Plus, their son, Matthew Santacoloma, who advises them on many social media topics, is hoping to join the team and work on Silent Partner's social media as well as sales—after working a job or two outside the family business first.

"Social media helps us to network so much more efficiently," Maria said. "In the old-school days of the dog-and-pony show of traditional networking, I might get to give a 30-second introduction during a two-hour lunch. On social media, I can reach 3,000 people in that same 30 seconds—from the comfort of my home."

Secrets to Our Success

Spread the word. "I'm always looking for places to leave my business cards," Maria said. "I've probably left my cards in every bathroom in the Lehigh Valley."

Wear a professional nametag. "I wear my nametag everywhere, even while running errands to Wegmans and Target," Maria said. "When people see it, they ask me questions about Medicare and AARP. Many seniors want to know about AARP and United because they are strong brands they trust!"

Strike up conversations. "Although Medicare salespeople are not allowed to just hand out a business card to someone, assuming they are of Medicare age, I can introduce the topic," Maria said. "If there's a long line at checkout, I'll joke 'It might be Medicare season by the time it's my turn.' That usually gets the conversation rolling. More often than not, they'll ask, 'Do you sell Medicare?' And *then* I can give them my card."

Give back. Silent Partner recently sponsored a program with an organization called Twilight Wish, which grants wishes for underprivileged seniors. "One man wished for dentures, and a lady wanted to go to a Phillies game," Maria said. "Another wanted to go on a picnic at a farm to see horses."

Work smart with family. The Santacolomas have been married for 25 years.

"We discuss all aspects of the business," Manny said. "We might have different opinions on some things, but we don't fight about them. We don't move ahead on anything major without talking with the other first."

"Although I do most of the talking though," Maria joked.

For More Information

- www.silentpartnerins.com
- 610-366-0124
- contact@silentpartnerins.com
- PO Box 32, Fogelsville, PA 18051
- Services offered: Medicare Supplement, Medicare Advantage, and Prescription Drug plans

Wicksquisite Candles

Handmade with HappYness

In high school, Latoya Hutchinson was always making people laugh, and her teachers would say, "One day, you'll be a stand-up comedian. You truly have a gift. I just wish you wouldn't perform in my class." She was only one vote shy of being voted class clown. To this day, she loves making people happy.

After graduation, Latoya attended college with a nursing major, which she chose because she had an interest in working with babies. She quickly realized becoming a nurse wasn't her calling and left school to enter the job force.

By the year 2018, Latoya was a single mom with two daughters and a son. She worked in sales over the years tying in her passion for connecting with people through humor. Latoya was excellent in sales but didn't want to do that type of work anymore. With three young children, a traditional 9-to-5 job took time away from them. "I promised myself I was going to attend my kids' activities and be present," she said.

During those difficult times of having to choose between being present for her children, maintaining financial stability, and finding a career that made sense for her life, Latoya said, "I felt like my life had no mission. It felt dark." Latoya spent much of her life around people with limited beliefs, who didn't support her ideas and dreams. "After you've been told enough times that you're not going to amount to anything, you start to believe it," she said.

One day while watching TV, she noticed many of the commercials were funny, and something clicked in her brain: *Comedy works to promote products because it's memorable.* Because she's naturally gifted at humor, Latoya realized a career in marketing would be a great fit. She could use her comedic gifts to promote products.

Latoya enrolled in Northampton Community College's marketing program. With the support of her new husband, Jeremey, Latoya attended classes year-round—each fall, spring, and summer—to accelerate her progress.

At left: Jeremey Hutchinson, Director of Operations; Latoya Hutchinson, Founder; Ava Collier, Marketing Assistant; Alyse Collier, Team Lead; and Jeremiah Palmer, Team Associate of Wicksquisite Candles

As Latoya's graduation neared, she started brainstorming the next step in her career that would support the flexible schedule she needed to remain present for her children. She researched "low-startup cost businesses." Soap-making was high on the list. She began watching YouTube videos to learn more. "I became obsessed with watching soap-making videos," she joked. "I figured I'd at least try it out. If nothing else, it would give me something to do with my kids over the summer."

The family's first project was creating rainbow Popsicle soaps, and then they advanced to more creative, whimsical soaps. When Latoya posted photos of her new creations on social media, her best friend, Yamelisa, made the first purchase and placed an order for her son's birthday. She quickly started getting messages from other parents, who wanted to buy them for party favors as well.

"Parents are more health conscious now," Latoya said. After fulfilling her first two soap orders, she told her husband, "I think this is what I want to do." She named her soap company Happyness Soaps. It was a meaningful tribute

Wicksquisite Candles's year-round top seller: their beach candle made with real sand and shells and made from a water-resembling gel wax

A custom-candle request for the "Diva Girls" women's poker club December 2022 and the most creative candle they've made to date: All pieces are hand created wax detail designs.

to her favorite movie *The Pursuit of Happyness,* a movie based on a true story about Chris Gardner, who struggled with homelessness while raising a toddler son and through dedication became a stockbroker.

"I raised my oldest daughter in a shelter for her first few months," Latoya explained. "Watching that movie was pivotal for me. It showed me that you can be dealt the most difficult hand and still rise." That message was so important to Latoya that she had "Happyness" tattooed on her wrist.

Latoya's soaps were extremely popular with friends and family and at craft fairs. At every show, at least one person asked if she made candles as well. When Latoya's husband heard about those requests, he told her, "Well, you might as well add candles too."

Latoya's first candles were simple, jarred candles. "They were so boring, I thought 'no candles for me,'" she joked. But as Latoya researched candle-making, she quickly realized there was great potential for making creative candles. Within a week, she was making coffee-style candles with whipped toppings.

At first, she hoped to make and sell *both* soap and candles. However, Latoya realized that she was able to get much more creative through her

Wicksquisite Candles's owner Latoya Hutchinson, making a batch of hazelnut vanilla iced coffee candles

candle designs and bring such joy to others. "I loved candles so much that soap was history," Latoya said. By January 2019, she stopped making soaps to make room for candles.

The name for Latoya's new company came to her in a dream: Wicksquisite Candles. As a nod to her former soap-making company, her tagline is Handmade with HappYness. Even though Latoya was sad to let go of soaps, she didn't stop making them entirely. She occasionally makes a batch.

As Wicksquisite Candles grew, Latoya looked to her family for help. Her husband is her best sounding-board. He's also a whiz with finances, and he handles much of the back-end office work.

Latoya's son, Jeremiah, comes up with new scent blends and combinations, such as Cranberry Apple Pumpkin. He also is her smell tester. No candles go out the door unless he approves. Her middle daughter, Alyse, is her out-of-the-box thinker, helping with candle ideas and candle-making workshops. Her oldest daughter, Ava, helps with marketing ideas and has been inspired by Latoya that she has now chosen marketing as her major. Latoya's third daughter, Alivia, is expected in 2024.

"My motto in 2023 was letting go of fear," Latoya said, a year that also brought her great business success. She entered a pitch competition—and won!

"Use your gifts to create your own happiness."

—Latoya Hutchinson

"That's when I knew that I was really doing something right," Latoya said. "My children and my business have pulled me out of some dark places in life. They've given me a reason to rise."

In the future, Latoya hopes to continue to grow their family business. She also plans to open her own candle-making studio, which will be the Lehigh Valley's first.

Secrets to Our Success

Surround yourself with people whose strengths are your weaknesses. Latoya heard this very message during one of her weakest times while listening to one of her favorite pastors T.D. Jakes. "I can tell you that it makes no sense to surround yourself with people who can do what you already know how to do." Latoya says. "It's much more beneficial to find people who can offer a different perspective and skills than those you already possess."

Do not measure success by profit. "People have a tendency to measure success by the amount of money they are making, instead of focusing on the original mission they were trying to fulfill. Stay focused on why you started, which is often not to make money. You had a passion!"

For More Information

Wicksquisite Candles

Handmade with Happyness

- www.WicksquisiteCandles.com

- 484-661-7281

- info@wicksquisitecandles.com

- Services offered: Handmade artisanal candle gifts, candle-making workshops, candle favors

Business Owners Trade Alliance

We Are a Family of Businesses Run by Partners in Business and Life

Business Owners Trade Alliance was founded by Scott Martz and Maria Wirth in 2010 with barter as a unique solution to help businesses thrive in any economic climate. As the region's largest barter company, they serve businesses of all types and sizes open to the strategy of organized business bartering. They currently have members throughout eastern and central Pennsylvania as well as New Jersey and other states.

When they meet people in business, they eventually ask, "Are you married?" The couple is not, but they have been together as partners in life and in business since 2011. Although it is a joy to find one's soulmate, it was tough in the beginning. Scott and Maria were both in relationships when they met and that was challenging in its own way.

Scott and Maria have been told that owning a business with a life partner can be taxing on the relationship if someone has a limited tolerance for time spent together with another person. "We are lucky in that we love spending time together!" Maria said. "Others have commented that they would never survive if they had to work with their spouse. For us, it's the opposite."

"Our backgrounds are quite different, but we have tremendous respect for one another," she added. "We know what we both bring to the table makes us a very effective team. Good times or bad, we have complete faith and trust that the other has our back."

Being a family business has certainly helped Scott and Maria to understand others on the same journey, and many of their members are like family. Their relationship with members is sometimes very close, and they have facilitated purchases for almost everything imaginable. They help convert cash expenses to trade, set up advertising, and direct people to qualified

At right: Scott Martz, CEO, and Maria Wirth, Managing Director, of Business Owners Trade Alliance

professionals for business services. They help to plan special dining experiences, weddings, vacations, birthdays, and anniversaries.

"We join members in celebrating company milestones and the birth of children," Maria said. "Having been in business as long as we have, we have also mourned with families at funerals. Although these are sad moments, we are proud to have known these members and been a part of their lives."

BOTA's barter community extends well beyond the Lehigh Valley and the surrounding region. They are part of a very large international group in the trade world, the International Reciprocal Trade Association. On this platform, there are 75,000 businesses in the United States alone engaging in trade with one another. Because of BOTA's heavy involvement in this marketplace and their strong financial position, they are fortunate to be able to refer their VIP members to very high level trade opportunities.

Scott Martz and Maria Wirth at their thirteenth annual trade show

Scott Martz and Maria Wirth showcasing their global trade opportunties

Secrets to Our Success

There are some key things that set BOTA apart other than being a family business. Many of their trading partners are also family run by husbands and wives, second generation, and extended family.

Keep it personal. "Although we embrace technology, using sophisticated barter software and other business tools, we are very hands-on and sensitive to our members' requests," Maria said. "We have grown strategically, believing our members should drive business development so they are not locked into purchasing what they don't need. Our members also transact business at regular pricing to cash customers and with few exceptions, everything is 100 percent trade. This makes our offers extremely competitive nationally and attractive from the standpoint of everyone involved getting the same fair deal."

"Since most businesses have never heard of what we do, it's exciting to share the type of products and services our members barter for every day," Maria continued. "We're really proud of this and the good we are able to do for members, and their employees and families. As you can see, many of these things are improving lives, not just making businesses stronger."

Major categories currently available on trade through BOTA include:

Scott Martz and Maria Wirth at one of their marketing events

Advertising, Marketing, and Website Development; Auto Services and Transportation; Business Products and Services; Cleaning; Construction; Grounds Maintenance and Landscaping; Health, Fitness and Beauty; Home and Family; Restaurants and Entertainment; Travel; Hotels and Resorts

Balance work and family. "With the nature of our business, we sometimes need to take calls and respond to emails after the workday is over," Maria said. "But we also try to step away from work when we can and take advantage of being able to run our business virtually. We are fortunate in that other than hosting and attending events, we can work from anywhere in the world. This allows us to take time for ourselves while running our business."

"We join members in celebrating company milestones and the birth of children. Having been in business as long as we have, we have also mourned with families at funerals. Although these are sad moments, we are proud to have known these members and been a part of their lives.
—Maria Wirth

Reap the rewards. "Sharing a life and raising children while running a business is not easy, but there have been incredible rewards," Maria stressed. "We would not trade one minute of our time together for something else or someone else. Depending on what happens in our kids' lives, they may someday own a business or want to work in the company. This is a very exciting prospect."

"Celebrating wins together is also very special," Maria added. "The other person really gets your enthusiasm about little things more than with couples who don't share a business."

"Last but not least, it's nice to have someone who is always there for you when you're having a tough day, someone who believes in you more than anyone in the world."

For More Information

- www.botatrade.com

- 610-222-5100

- info@botatrade.com

- 3440 Lehigh Street, Suite 228, Allentown, PA 18103

- Services offered: The benefits of buying and selling with trade dollars instead of cash. Members enjoy bartering purchasing power with participating local businesses and a marketplace with over 75,000 members.

BusinessOwners
TRADE ALLIANCE
THE REGION'S LARGEST BARTER SOURCE
WWW.BOTATRADE.COM

Increasing the Visibility of Your Family Business

Open Door Public Relations—Rita Guthrie

Rita Guthrie started her consulting business by accident. She recalled, "A few decades back, I served on the board of a small nonprofit arts organization. Wow. That sounds like a lifetime ago." Admitting that brevity isn't her strong suit, she struggled to give me the nutshell version of her backstory. "Any community organization's board needs people with complementary strengths: leadership, programming, fundraising, bookkeeping, and recruiting and retaining members. The years serving on this board brought out skills that I never knew I had: The power and ability to conjure up creative marketing ideas on the fly. Who knew? When the leadership team got stuck on an issue, someone would say, 'I don't know. Ask the Idea Lady.'"

The organization's logo was weak, amateurish, and outdated. They needed an updated image. There was little room in the budget to hire a professional (maybe $100, at best). The Idea Lady blurted out, "Let's conduct a logo design contest!" But, how? (Keep in mind that in the 1990s, social media wasn't a thing.) Rita reached out to every local news and arts publication imaginable with

Rita Guthrie speaking at Penn State on Pitching: The Art of Persuasion

At left: Rita Guthrie, owner of Open Door Public Relations

The time that Rita asked for everyone's nametag

a press release describing the rules, criteria, and deadline for the contest. "We had about thirty submissions, some were even hand-drawn by young art students. It turned out that the winner was a retired graphic designer. Talk about an excellent return on investment (ROI). For $100 in prize money, we were blessed with a professional logo design that represented us quite well. And the bonus was added publicity for the organization."

Over time, Rita reluctantly responded to occasional requests from her board colleagues to put her brainstorming finesse to work in helping their friends. They would have a great business concept but no clue how to get the word out. After a few such referrals, Rita decided to get business cards printed.

"They were awful, by the way," Rita laughed. So, in 2005 the Idea Lady was born.

Around the same time, Rita attended a fundraiser for public television at PBS-39 featuring Barbara Sher, an inspirational speaker and author of several books, including *Wishcraft: How to Get What You Really Want*. When she wasn't busy doing *60 Minutes* or *Oprah*, Ms. Sher traveled around the country doing "Dare to Soar Summits" and encouraged her followers to create local events called "Idea Parties." But the closest one was in Doylestown, Pennsylvania. During the Q&A, Rita stood to ask Ms. Sher if she would need specific training or permission to start an Idea Party in the Lehigh Valley. Her response was, "No. Go for it!" So Rita turned to the audience and said, "If you would like me to contact you, write your email on your nametag and stick it to my blazer on your way out." They did. "I had about twenty-five nametags stuck all over me and had some meaningful discussions with the other attendees. It was weird to see such positive results from what was an off-the-cuff idea."

Within a few weeks, Rita organized her first gathering at a local library. There were about a dozen attendees. One of them, a dentist, became her first official consulting client. "Thank goodness he didn't know that he was my first," Rita chuckled.

And that was the beginning of her monthly events now known as Coffee Talk.

Almost two decades later, Rita is well known in the small business community as a congenial and perceptive small business consultant focusing on challenges in marketing and business relations. Of the thousands of small business owners Rita has advised over the years, many of them began as, or eventually became, a family business. That was the inspiration for this, our third collaborative book in the Local Luminaries Series.

How Do We Define a Family Business?

A family business is one owned or operated by spouses, parents and children, siblings, or any combination of relatives. A family business can also be one that has been handed down through generations.

Among the chapters in this book, you'll find Edwing Joseph's story (page 80). He learned about creating and tailoring fine suits from observing his father's skills and went on to establish his business as *Edwing Joseph & Sons*, looking toward a future of including his young children.

Jimmy Olang was employed by the original *Brothers That Just Do Gutters* in New York's Hudson Valley before he and his wife, Jessi, became the first Brothers Gutters franchisees (page 62). They now mentor some of the other 150+ franchisees across the country. The Olangs have worked hard to grow their business to the multi-million-dollar success that it is today, and they have added other family members to the team.

Audra Frank (page 32) and her late husband, David, bought his father's painting business. After many years of growing the enterprise, keeping up with trends in the industry and developing a top-notch reputation, Audra lost David to cancer. Being a woman

Rita Guthrie is a sought-after speaker at business events and colleges.

"Five Steps to Killer Marketing" is one of the many workshops that Rita Guthrie presents.

of strength and determination, she carried on with the family business as *AFA Renovate* and continues to have a golden reputation for fine work and using green products in her renovations and redesigns. Her sense of humor adds to the fun of working with her.

Billboards and Speeches

Ten years ago, Rita began consulting with Kim Semmel of *Dance with Kim* (page 56). "Miss Kim" had secured time on a billboard and needed input as to what information and images to display. Her biggest problem was that she loved all of her dance families and wanted to show that love, and the studio contact details, on the billboard. After the realization that people zooming past the sign would only have time to glance at it, they had to develop messaging that was easily absorbed. What Rita advised was to include three simple photos, side-by-side, showing a tiny dancer, a dance team, and a teen soloist, captioned with the website. It was a great summary of what was offered at Kim's studio.

A few years later, Rita received a panicked call from Kim saying something like, "OMG! I have to give a speech! I need help! I'm a dancer, not a speaker!" Apparently, Kim had arranged for her dancers to perform for a local charity fundraiser for many years. The organization was honoring Kim with an award to show their appreciation. But she had to give an acceptance speech. Fortunately, Rita was accustomed to working with her clients in many aspects of public speaking. During their meetings, Rita observed Kim's body language go from clenched apprehension to relaxed confidence as they worked together to develop an outline, including language that was gracious, authentic, and comfortable for Kim.

At the time, Kim's teen daughter, Brittany, was a dance student at the Charter Arts High School, as well as a member of the faculty at *Dance with Kim*. Now "Miss Brittany" is the studio's co-director. She is also married with her own little dancing daughter.

Kicking Your Marketing up a Notch

When a new client brings on Rita as their marketing and business relations consultant, she does her homework. Before their first official consultation, she scans their website and socials and Googles them to learn a bit about the owners and the company. The meeting begins with Rita reflecting back to the owners what she's learned. The ideal response to that would be, "Great! That's exactly what I want people to know about our business." But more often than not, the response is, "Oops!" Or, "That's out of date." Rita's review also looks for brand consistency, so that their website is aligned with their signage, social media pages, handouts/menus, T-shirts, name badges, etc. It is valuable for a business to have their public-facing content be reviewed by an outsider to assure that they have a strong, memorable, recognizable brand identity.

Essential Marketing and Public Relations Tips from the Idea Lady

Brand identity

Know what constitutes your brand. Your logo, fonts, colors, design, and images are all valuable elements of your brand. But it is much more than that. It is the feeling people get when they enter your office, shop, restaurant, or website. Setting the atmosphere and expectations is vital. It is the vibe and general messaging offered in your marketing materials and social media presence. It includes your reputation, reviews, referrals, and customer service. And don't forget to include your appearance, personality, confidence, and attitude. You want make your clients feel great!

Making your story relatable

One of the golden secrets of marketing is to have a great origin story, one that makes your business truly relatable to your prospective clients. Don't be afraid to be funny or poignant. The *about us* page on your website or social media should give your readers some insight into how your business got started, your company's philosophy, and why you are

Rita Guthrie is a strong advocate of business networking.

passionate about what you do. Be enthusiastic and engaging, and speak about how you *love* your work.

Images tell the story

It's a well-known fact that social media posts, print media, and websites add value and get the message across super-fast when accompanied by images. It just attracts more engagement. Photos can include head shots, staff members in action, a pleased client, or images of your business's space, products or services. Marketing photos fall into three categories: professional photography, snapshots and selfies, and stock photography. They all serve the purpose of underscoring your brand identity, telling a story with more visual and less written content, and increasing the know-like-trust factor.

But wait. There's more. You can include a map for directions, a chart to show intersectionality, or a graph to depict statistics and measurable accomplishments. Whether factual or funny, instructional or educational, these visual tools provide more information with a simple glance.

Educate, Entertain, Engage

Rita often uses this strategy with her consulting clients: Adding one more layer with a new idea or fresh perspective to what you are already doing. She helps you pivot just slightly for increased visibility from your marketing activities. It doesn't have to be a complete reinvention of your business.

And when it comes to your marketing plan, especially in social media, the Idea Lady accentuates three key communication goals in creating meaningful posts: educate, entertain, and engage. When your content adds value, you are more likely to engage your target audience.

Educate: Share valuable information and knowledge that shows your followers how to level up their lives. Sharing your wisdom and expertise, in small doses, can help tremendously to stand out from your competition.

Instead of using posts meant to sell your product or service, try offering tips that add value or bits of information that arouse curiosity. For example, you can educate your followers on the latest fashion, updates in insurance coverage, or your special menu items created from what is in season. Have you noticed Shawn Doyle, of Savory Grille (page 14), on TV or at a public event giving a cooking demonstration? Not only is he a brilliant chef, but his charming smile and the appearance of deliciousness attract positive attention. Adam Gangewere and Elizabeth Ortiz of Cactus Blue (page 8) have been posting amazing photos of and talking about their featured menu items. And

Almost two decades later, Rita is well known in the small business community as a congenial and perceptive small business consultant focusing on challenges in marketing and business relations.

everybody loves before and after photos when you get in shape, renovate a property, or add a beautiful feature to your home.

Entertain: Talk about fails, funny situations, and misunderstandings, that is if you are including the lesson learned, why it was hilarious, or how that situation led to a new product or income stream. Create fun videos. We all know that the most entertaining or humorous videos get shared. That's valuable. The memes and messages that you post do not have to be related directly to your business. Show your fun side, but keep within the flavor of your brand identity.

You can host a co-marketing event with a complementary business that deals with the same demographic as you. Have fun with it and talk about what's happening on social media before, during, and after the experience.

Engage: What type of interactions are you getting from your posts? Track your social media pages for likes, comments, and shares. Ask for opinions and feedback. Stay in touch with your clients and fans by continuously building your mailing list and offering valuable content. Host business events and run workshops. And give valuable referrals to other business owners whenever the opportunity presents itself.

Every interaction, every conversation, builds the know-like-trust factor essential to growing your network of fans and followers.

For More Information

- www.opendoorlv.com

- 610-703-5878

- idealady@opendoorlv.com

- Services offered: Small business consulting focusing on public relations and marketing, developing strategies to increase visibility in the marketplace. Assessment of marketing materials for clarity and consistency. Creating a call-to-action: getting customers to cross your threshold or make that call.

ABOUT THE
Photographer

Terree O'Neill Oakwood is a professional photographer and entrepreneur. Twenty-eight years ago, she began The Moment Photography, creating studio and location lifestyle and branding portraits. Terree also enjoys dabbling in writing and has chronicled on Facebook the many life changes she has experienced in recent years. In so doing, she's discovered her enjoyment of inspiring others through the stories of simple life happenings. Next on her list, she hopes to combine her photography and love of writing into a book that would help others notice the wonder all around us and grow from an open-hearted approach to living.

ABOUT THE
Curators

Jennifer Bright

Jennifer is founding CEO of Bright Communications LLC.

Jennifer is a publisher, editor, and writer with more than 25 years of publishing experience. She has contributed to more than 150 books and published more than 100 magazine and newspaper articles.

She proudly served as a lieutenant in the U.S. Army for four years, stationed at Fort Lewis, Washington. Jennifer then worked for seven years on staff at Rodale before launching her own editorial business, Bright Communications LLC.

Jennifer's passion is helping authors bring their books to life. She lives in Hellertown, Pennsylvania, with her two sons and two cats. She can be reached at jennifer@brightcommunications.net.

Rita Guthrie

Rita, founder of Open Door Public Relations, has been involved in marketing, public relations, and creative business events since the early 90s. Back in the day, her colleagues nicknamed her the Idea Lady for being the go-to person for brainstorming clever PR and marketing ideas.

Open Door PR was established in 2005 with a focus on small business and start-ups. As a business-to-business consultant, Rita has helped thousands of clients increase their visibility and bottom line by seeing through the clutter and giving them what they really need. She has a flair for making valuable connections for her clients and adds remarkably simple layers to what her clients are already doing to increase the value of and response to their marketing efforts. The Idea Lady helps the business owner explore a wide variety of tools to reach out, stay in touch, and arouse the curiosity of prospective clients. She feels that all small businesses should look at how they educate, entertain, and engage their prospective clients.

In addition to one-to-one consulting, Rita runs monthly Coffee Talks with various public relations or marketing themes. Essentially, they are discussion-based networking events. She has a genuine love of connecting people and seeing small businesses grow and flourish.

Rita is a sought-after speaker with a conversational style that engages her audiences right from the onset of her presentations.

A native of Brooklyn, she also lived Upstate New York and at the Jersey Shore before coming to the Lehigh Valley in 1987. Rita and her husband have three children and five grandchildren. She practices yoga and catches up on NPR podcasts during her daily walks. Rita can be reached at idealady@opendoorlv.com.

Robert Sayre

Rob, a native of Boulder, Colorado moved to the East Coast in 1982 to work at a small book publishing Company in New York City and then to the Lehigh Valley in 1988 to work at Rodale, Inc. as the business manager of its book division. He worked with Bob Rodale and many other great leaders and coworkers.

Rob's children are grown, but he never left the Lehigh Valley. Now semi-retired, he is an active investor in real estate and a volunteer as a master gardener with the Penn State Extension Service. He has studied and practiced tai chi for thirteen years. Rob is also an advisor on housing issues with Community Action of the Lehigh Valley (CALV).

He and his wife, Sally, a retired public-school teacher, have three children and five exceptional grandchildren. They are as busy as ever, but they love controlling their own schedule and traveling in their Lance RV Camper. You can reach Rob at robert.sayre1@gmail.com.

We appreciate the continued
support of First United Land Transfer
www.FirstUnitedClosing.com
610-433-0432

 @FirstUnitedClosing

 @FirstUnitedClosing

We appreciate the continued support of

Venture X Bethlehem

Gateway at Greenway Park,

306 S New St, Bethlehem, PA 18015

610-839-8109

Also in the Local Luminaries Series

Do you want to create a Local Luminaries edition for your community?

Email Jennifer@BrightCommunications.net to learn how!

www.ingramcontent.com/pod-product-compliance
Lightning Source LLC
Chambersburg PA
CBHW051317120626
46547CB00015B/2278